Start Your Own

AUTOMOBILE DETAILING BUSINESS

Additional titles in *Entrepreneur's* **Startup Series**

Start Your Own

Bar and Tavern

Bed & Breakfast

Business on eBay

Business Support Service

Car Wash

Child Care Service

Cleaning Service

Clothing Store

Coin-Operated Laundry

Consulting

Crafts Business

e-Business

e-Learning Business

Event Planning Business

Executive Recruiting Service

Freight Brokerage Business

Gift Basket Service

Growing and Selling Herbs and Herbal Products

Home Inspection Service

Import/Export Business

Information Consultant Business

Lawn Care Business

Mail Order Business

Medical Claims Billing Service

Personal Concierge Service

Personal Training Business

Pet-Sitting Business

Restaurant and Five Other Food Businesses

Self-Publishing Business

Seminar Production Business

Specialty Travel & Tour Business

Staffing Service

Successful Retail Business

Vending Business

Wedding Consultant Business

Wholesale Distribution Business

Entrepreneur®
MAGAZINE'S

startup

Start Your Own

AUTOMOBILE DETAILING BUSINESS

Your Step-by-Step Guide to Success

Entrepreneur Press and Eileen Figure Sandlin

EP
Entrepreneur
Press

Editorial Director: Jere L. Calmes
Managing Editor: Marla Markman
Cover Design: Beth Hansen-Winter
Production: Eliot House Productions
Composition: Ed Stevens

This publication is designed to provide accurate and authoritative information in regard
to the subject matter covered. It is sold with the understanding that the publisher is not
engaged in rendering legal, accounting or other professional services. If legal advice or
other expert assistance is required, the services of a competent professional person should
be sought.

Library of Congress Cataloging-in-Publication Data is available

ISBN 1-932531-41-6

Printed in Canada

11 10 09 08 07 06 05   10 9 8 7 6 5 4 3 2 1

Contents

▲

Preface

It's a "dirty" job, but somebody's got to do it...and now that you've made the decision to be a professional automobile detailer, you could be the one who turns water into dollar signs.

Automobile detailing has been a hot industry for enterprising entrepreneurs for more than a decade. Some experts believe the trend toward detailing as a profession was spawned by the sharp spike in new-car sticker prices that began in the '80s, which induced thrifty Americans to hold onto their vehicles way past their expiration date. Others think the industry was spawned by the entrepreneurial spirit that gripped America throughout the '90s, persuading frazzled 9-to-5ers to escape from high-stress jobs and plunge into self-employment ventures that didn't force them to sacrifice their quality of life. Still others feel detailing has evolved into a popular start-up business simply because the initial costs are fairly low and the potential for profit is as high as the detailer's ambition.

Ambition is just one of the traits a new automotive detailer needs for success. Meticulous attention to detail, patience, and a gift of gab also come in handy. A genuine love of anything with horses under the hood and four on the floor doesn't hurt, either.

Since running your own business means you'll be responsible for everything from obtaining financing to paying the bills, it also helps to have at least a basic aptitude for numbers, even if your experience consists only of balancing your checkbook accurately and reviewing your personal investment statements. Previous high school or college coursework in disciplines like accounting and business management helps even more. But don't be concerned if your education has been a little light on financial know-how. Between the business professionals who can help keep your books and do your taxes and your own motivation, you can be successful in this field.

In this book, we've given you all the practical advice you'll need to build an automotive detailing business from the chassis up. That includes information you'll need to handle the myriad details that go into starting and operating a small business—from analyzing your market, writing a business plan, and establishing an internet presence to finding financing and handling all the other day-to-day duties necessary to keep your business running like a well-oiled machine. There are worksheets to help you calculate costs, keep expenditures under control, and stay organized. There also are names and addresses (both snail and cyber) of numerous industry organizations, suppliers, and government agencies that can provide answers and ideas.

But perhaps most important, there are words of wisdom throughout this book from auto detailers and industry experts who have unique insight into the behind-the-scenes process of running a professional detailing business. What's more, they've all agreed to be personal resources for you in case you have questions that only another detailer can answer. You'll find contact information for these industry professionals in the Appendix.

And incidentally, what you won't find in these pages is instructions for buffing paint to a mirror finish or removing swirls. Frankly, that instruction is best left to the pros who teach detailing techniques, including the companies that make the detailing chemicals you'll be using. You'll find information about instructional opportunities in Chapter 9 and in the Appendix.

Because people come into this industry with different resources and expectations, we've covered techniques for starting a business both on a shoestring and on a budget supercharged with cash. So now, let's put the pedal to the metal and shift into gear. This is gonna be the ride of your life!

1

Start Your
Engines

When it comes to an industry with wide-open opportunities for enterprising small-business owners, auto detailing ranks right up there with the best of them.

And small wonder. Americans' passion for cars, coupled with busy, fast-paced lifestyles that leave them with little time to take care of those vehicles properly, has created an environment rife with potential for today's aspiring detailer. Just consider this: A recent survey by carlove.org indicated that 84 percent of American car owners love or like their cars, but only 15 percent of those take excellent care of the object of their affection. Does that mean the other 69 percent could be your customers? You bet! In fact, the 2002 International Carwash Association *Study of Consumer Car Washing Attitudes and Habits* showed that 42 percent of exterior carwash customers would wash their cars more often if they were offered a "portering" option (12 percent), if they had more time (17 percent), or if it took less time (13 percent). A professional detailer can meet all these requirements.

> **Bright Idea**
> A lot of people don't know the difference between detailing (restoring) and customizing (adding nifty extras like fancy wheels). Be sure to explain exactly what you do in your promotional materials and Yellow Pages ad.

The Big Picture

Despite the detailing industry's enormous earning potential and small-business opportunities, there is surprisingly little information available about it in terms of statistics and trends. The industry doesn't have its own professional association (the closest thing is the International Carwash Association, which has a detailing component). What little statistical information is available on the numbers of detailers, wages, and other pertinent information is several years old. Even the federal government doesn't pay much attention to the profession (except for the IRS, that is). Detailers aren't singled out in the Bureau of Labor Statistics' *Occupational Outlook Handbook* (published by the U.S. Department of Labor); rather, they're included in the "Equipment Cleaners, Helpers, and Laborers" category (which no doubt includes those who clean everything from industrial manufacturing machinery to dry cleaning equipment). Likewise, the Bureau of the Census has a similar "Cleaners of Vehicles and Equipment" category, which presumably includes carwash employees. But the Census Bureau offers no other information about these employees the way it does for hair stylists, longshoremen, and other professionals.

"There's not a lot of official recognition for this profession and no statistics," confirms auto reconditioning expert Prentice St. Clair, owner of Detail in Progress in San Diego. "That's probably because it's such an easy business to get into that three-quarters of the businesses are 'under the radar.'"

According to the latest statistics available from *Professional Carwashing & Detailing* magazine, there are more than 8,000 independent detailers in the United States. According to R. L. "Bud" Abraham, owner of Detail Plus Car Appearance Systems of Portland, Oregon, and one of the detailing industry's top experts, today there are nearly 14,000 detailers in the Yellow Pages, which is a 71 percent increase over the number in 1980. In addition, there were 15,000 carwashes in 1980, 10 percent of which did detailing. Today, nearly 85 percent of the nation's 17,000 carwashes do some form of detailing. Considering there were nearly 130 million passenger cars on the road in 2002, according to R. L. Polk, a Detroit consumer research company, that's not a lot of detailers to go around. So the outlook for success in this industry is excellent.

Historical Perspective

Although detailing came into its own as an industry fairly recently, the profession actually dates back to the days of the horse-drawn carriage, which were lovingly hand polished and spit-shined. But it really gathered steam with the advent of vehicles that had the horses under rather than in front. One of the pioneers in what would become the detailing product industry was furniture polish maker Frank Meguiar Jr., who, in 1901, mixed bottles of wood polish one at a time using an eggbeater. He soon realized that his product also could be used on those early automobiles, which were made of wood and coated with the same finishes used on furniture, and a new industry was born.

Until the 1940s, owners of elite motorcars were the most frequent consumers of detailing services. Then, after World War II, car dealership owners realized that reconditioning previously owned cars would increase their value and thereby increase the dealers' profit margins. As a result, many dealerships added full-service detailing departments, which soon were prepping new cars for delivery. But the recessions of 1980 and 1982 forced many dealers to reduce or lay off their detailing staff, which opened the door to new opportunities for independent detailers.

Not coincidentally, the consumer detailing market started to heat up around the same time. As cars became more expensive, consumers started keeping their vehicles for longer periods of time. In 1969, for example, when the average price of a new car was $3,708, consumers kept their cars an average of 6.4 years. By 2001, there were 216 million vehicles in use (40 percent of which were trucks), and the average price of a new car had increased to $14,449. Likewise, the length of time consumers kept their cars increased to an average of nine years. Now that the average sticker price for a new car or light truck hit $30,481 in December 2003, according to an analysis by auto price tracker Edmunds.com, consumers will probably be even more likely to keep parking their same old cars and trucks in the garage.

Another factor also influenced Americans' predilection to keep their cars longer: The fed eral government erased the tax deduction for auto loan and credit card interest in the '80s. Suddenly, a new car loan was an even greater liability than before, and people started looking

Stat Fact
Men drove 65 percent more miles than women in 2001, down from 126 percent more in 1977, according to the U.S. Department of Energy.

at their trusty old cars with infinitely more fondness. Take a look at the chart below and the one on page 5, which illustratehow many miles people are driving annually and how long they are keeping their cars.

All this thriftiness represents a great opportunity for a new detailer. Many owners of older vehicles want to keep their rides in top condition, particularly those vehicles that have weathered a couple of presidential administrations. But keep in mind that people who wash their cars at home in the driveway are not likely to be your customers. The 2002 International Carwash Association *Study of Consumer Car Washing Attitudes and Habits* indicated that nearly 86 percent of home washers who responded to the survey had not had their car detailed in the previous year. So your challenge will be to find the consumers who take pride in their vehicles but don't have the time or inclination to keep them looking showroom-ready.

Earning Potential

Although there aren't many hard and fast statistics about the scope and size of the detailing industry, it's easy to do the math to figure out what your potential earnings could be. Let's say you charge $185 for a full interior/exterior detailing. Detail five cars a week, and you'd earn $925 before taxes and expenses. At that pace, your gross revenue would be $48,100 per year. Promote extra services like paintless dent repair, vinyl and leather repair, and paint touch-up, and you can easily get the price of a detailing up to $400 or more. Detail just one extra car a week at $400, and you'd add nearly $21,000 to your gross revenue. That's $69,100 gross for a total of just six cars a week, 52 weeks a year.

Average Annual Miles Driven		
Year	Males	Females
1969	11,352	5,411
1977	13,397	5,940
1983	13,962	6,382
1990	16,536	9,528
1995	16,555	10,144
2001	16,749	10,174

Source: U.S. Department of Energy

Some detailers make even more. One California mobile detailer we know of, who has eight employees, has had annual sales as high as $250,000. On the other hand, *Professional Carwashing & Detailing* magazine says the hourly pay for a detailer ranges from $15 to $75, and National Detail Systems, which sells auto detailing and reconditioning systems, estimates an independent detailer can earn $30 to $60 an hour, or $1,000 to $1,500 a week, by detailing two cars a day. The amount you can earn is probably somewhere in the middle, but make no mistake: The sky's the limit for a new detailing professional.

The Opportunities

There are three types of detailing operations: Mobile, express, and site-based. Mobile businesses are the quickest and easiest type to launch, since all you have to do is buy some professional equipment and chemicals, as well as a van or trailer to haul that around in, and take to the road. This is also the most cost-effective way to enter the business, as there's no overhead other than the cost of your professional products and your vehicle, and no mortgage or lease payment. Instead, you work in parking lots, at office complexes, at customers' homes, and possibly in your own garage.

Express detailers often work in carwashes or at auto dealerships. This is a "while you wait" type of business—vehicle owners turn over their keys and wheels so you can do your magic, then get back a sparkling clean vehicle in a set period of time—say, 15 minutes. Although both carwashes and auto dealerships sometimes have their own detailing staff, there are many opportunities to work as a subcontractor at these businesses. And the arrangement is usually pure profit—the owner is usually so thrilled to have someone on site that there's no fee for the use of the space and utilities. This is

Average Number of Years of Ownership

Type of Vehicle	1969	1977	1990	1995	2001
Automobile	6.4	7.2	7.6	8.2	9.0
Pickup	7.3	8.5	8.4	9.7	10.1
SUV				6.7	6.5
Van	5.5	8.5	5.9	6.7	7.6
All Vehicles	6.6	7.6	7.7	8.3	8.9

Note: SUVs were not specifically named in the survey until 1995.
Source: U.S. Department of Transportation

Stat Fact

After plunging from a high of 36 percent of new-vehicle business in 1998, the vehicle leasing market is on the rise again and could be 21 percent in 2004, up from 19 percent the previous year, according to CNW Marketing Research, a Bandon, Oregon, market research company. The increase is attributable to rising interest rates and a reduction in the number of available low-mileage used cars.

particularly true of dealerships, where perfect appearance is paramount when it comes to high-priced new and used cars.

Industry experts say that the average price of an express detailing at a carwash is $36, including the carwash. The labor rate for the detailing is just 20 percent, and supplies are just a few dollars, so the profits can be very tidy, indeed, considering how little time is necessary to do the work.

"I think this is the direction the detailing industry is heading," says Dave Echnoz of 14/69 Carwash Supercenter in Fort Wayne, Indiana. "Twenty minutes, no appointment—it's great for someone who can't be without a car or doesn't want to rent a vehicle."

Fixed-location detailers work out of a building dedicated to detailing. Their overhead is certainly higher than that of a mobile or express detailer, but they have a distinct advantage over the mobile folks: a roof over their heads, so inclement weather that would shut down a mobile detailer is never a problem. With that roof comes a mortgage or lease payment, property taxes, overhead, and myriad other costs. But the trade-off is that site-based detailers can make a lot of money—as much as six figures or more, depending on the size of the operation. If you're lucky, you might be able to find a detailing shop or service station up for sale that already has all the tools and toys you need, like service bays and professional equipment. If not, you'll have to remodel, but the trade-off is that the finished shop will be exactly the way you want it. Incidentally, some site-based detailers offer express services for customers who are in a hurry. The most common express services are waxing and carpet cleaning.

There's one other type of detailing operation that bears mentioning. Detailing franchises offer another quick way to get into business with a minimum of effort (and cash) upfront. These turnkey operations provide you with an established name, which gives you an instant reputation; resources to help you do business, including advertising and marketing tools and assistance; and sometimes even equipment like mobile trailers. The franchise fees for these operations vary, but they can run tens of thousands of dollars—which can be about as much as establishing your own site-based detail shop would be. For the purposes of this book, we will assume that you are starting your own business from scratch, but just in case you're interested in franchises, you'll find some listed in the Appendix.

The Challenge

Now your mission, should you choose to accept it, is to find the people who have disposable income they're willing to part with and all-American pride in their vehicles, as well as automotive professionals who prefer to subcontract the work rather than having detailers on staff. Among the potential prospects are:

- Average Joe (and Josie) consumers who are in love with their cars (carlove.org says 64 percent of car owners talk to their cars and 27 percent give them pet names, so you know they're out there)
- White-collar professionals with high profiles (including but not limited to physicians, lawyers, and corporate executives)
- Sports car owners (to whom appearance is everything—including under the hood)
- People who lease cars (since a professional detailing can reduce the chance of incurring ghastly end-of-lease wear-and-tear charges)
- Show car/classic car owners/car buffs who show off their vehicles for love . . . and money
- New and used vehicle dealerships (the pace can be grueling and the work doesn't always pay top dollar, but there's usually a lot of work for a new detailer)
- People who are selling their own cars in the local classifieds (currently a huge untapped market)
- RV dealerships and their customers (still another gold mine of possibilities)
- Automotive centers like auto malls
- Carwashes (usually as an express detailing operation)
- Auto repair shops (including collision shops)
- Limousine companies
- Hotels with concierge service that might want to offer detailing as a premium service to guests
- Gas stations/garages that offer complete automotive services

Other prospects include boat and airplane owners (gotta look "fly" as they cast off or taxi away from the terminal) and railroad companies (don't worry—Meguiar's has you covered with the appropriate train polish). Many detailers start with cars, then segue into other types of vehicle detailing as a way to keep busy when the weather is poor. This type of detailing work is also a wide open market for entrepreneurs.

So are you ready to clean up in this promising industry? Great. Then turn the page so we can get your new business cranked up.

Fun Fact

The first automatic carwash in the United States opened in Detroit in 1946.

The Well-Oiled
Business Machine

Although there's a lot more to starting a detailing business than buying a bunch of powerful car toys (e.g., buffers and extractors) and playing with professional-grade products, we know you're dying to start dyeing and polishing. So this chapter will focus on the different maintenance and restoration services a detailer can provide, as well as the day-to-day functions involved in running the business.

One of the first things you should do in the process of setting up a detailing business is to determine exactly which services you'd like to perform. If you've been an amateur detailer ever since you got your first set of wheels, you already have a pretty good idea what a detailer does, as well as how long it takes to do it. But just in case you've never detailed a car before, or it's been years since you've had time to pamper your own chrome cruiser, let's take a look at the many services a detailer can offer.

Cleaning Up

Among the basic exterior detailing services are:

- Hand wash (with particular attention to tree sap, bug remains, bird droppings, and rail dust)
- Hand dry, usually with chamois or another soft, lint-free cloth
- Claying to remove all surface contaminants from the paint after the vehicle is washed
- Hand application of wax or sealant
- Application of wax using an orbital buffer
- Window and exterior mirror cleaning
- Trim and tire dressing application and polishing
- Wheel/rim waxing

Regular interior detailing services include:

- Floor and seat vacuuming (including vacuuming with a crevice tool for deep penetration)
- Floor and seat shampooing
- Cleaning and dressing of dashboard, door panels, and center console
- Vent, kick panel, pedal, doorjamb, and ashtray cleaning
- Floor mat vacuuming and steam cleaning
- Headliner cleaning
- Leather seat and trim cleaning and conditioning
- Vinyl seat cleaning and dressing
- Window and mirror cleaning and polishing

It's not necessary to offer every service on these lists as part of your regular interior or exterior detailing. Rather, you'll need to create the right combination of services that will maximize your profits while keeping labor costs firmly in check. For instance, you may find it's sufficient to vacuum a vehicle's interior thoroughly rather than shampooing the carpet as part of every interior detailing. Or perhaps steam cleaning is enough to freshen up a vehicle's interior. You'll need to make that determination based on factors like local weather conditions and the expectations created by your competition.

Detailers typically offer a wide range of additional services as a way to earn more money per vehicle. Often, these upgraded services are part of special packages concocted by the detailer to address different maintenance and restoration issues. Among these upgraded services are:

- Engine detailing (including degreasing and washing the engine, doorjambs, and hoses; cleaning under the hood and motor compartment)

- Trunk cleaning (vacuuming the interior, washing the jambs)

- Undercarriage detailing (removing road salt, dirt, and tar from the underbody and wheels, painting of wheels, applying undercoat)

- Scotchguard®, UV sealer applications for upholstery

- Carpeting and upholstery dyeing

- Trim and instrumentation repairs

- Odor removal and deodorizing

- Ozone odor removal

- Exterior Teflon® sealant

- Compounding and polishing to remove oxidation, scratches, scuffs, swirl marks, minor scratches, water spots, and stains

- Convertible top care

- Windshield wiper replacement

> **Smart Tip** *Tip...*
>
> Using the proper equipment and chemicals will help you complete your work more efficiently and in less time. Case in point: Lint-free towels or chamois may cost more, but you won't have to worry about fibers clinging to a vehicle's paint finish when you're ready to start waxing.

Finally, there are several specialty add-on services you can offer that will really beef up your bottom line. The services not only will maximize the amount you can earn on every vehicle you detail, but also they can be very lucrative profit centers in themselves. However, some of these services require hands-on training before you go to town on someone's vehicle so you don't inadvertently cause damage. Among the popular add-ons are:

- Custom paint touch-up, chip and scratch repair

- Black trim restoration

- Carpet and upholstery dyeing

- Vinyl and leather repair

- Windshield repair and tinting

- Paintless dent repair

- Overspray or cement removal

Obviously, not every detailer will be able to offer all these services. In fact, the prospect of offering so many services can be downright scary for some people. Often the decision about what you'll offer will be dependent on the size of your facility and whether you can afford the equipment when you start out. On the mobile side, you might have to limit your services simply because you have to carry every piece of equipment and every product you'll need with you on the road, including water tanks, spray equipment, and other devices. Some of the specialty services require equipment that's just not portable enough for a mobile detailer who's already carrying so much stuff—unless, of course, you plan to invest in a *really* big rig.

> **Smart Tip** *Tip...*
>
> There's no need to be secretive when you're collecting information about your competitors. With 130 million cars on the road, there's plenty of business to go around, and most competitors will welcome the opportunity to exchange ideas and war stories with another professional in the field.

Although it's not unusual for detailers to offer à la carte services, especially if the market is smaller and more price-sensitive, it's actually more common to offer packages of services as a way to make vehicles—and your bottom line—really shine. The cost for a package is usually less than the cost of the individual services combined, which is perceived as a better value by the customer. For instance, a complete bumper-to-fender detailing package might include hand wash and wax services, from deep cleaning of interior surfaces to engine and trunk detailing. A buffing and compounding package to remove surface scratches and swirls would start with a full wash and wax followed by custom paint chip and scratch repair.

Here's an example of what a full detail package might include:

- Hand wash and dry
- Claying, buffing, and waxing
- Deep cleaning (shampooing) of interior surfaces, including carpets and mats, and leather or vinyl upholstery conditioning
- Dressing of tires/wheels cleaned and polished
- Engine compartment and trunk detailing

For a package like this, you could charge anywhere from $125 to $225, depending on what the market will bear. (Large metro markets like Los Angeles could be even more.) Naturally, oversized vehicles like SUVs and trucks would cost more. (One detailer we know charges 20 percent more for oversized vehicles.)

So how do you know what to include in your packages? One way to make a determination is to check out what your competitors are doing. Certainly, some services beyond basic washing and waxing should be standard in your packages, like carpet and mat cleaning and interior dressing. But you can make a splash among the other detailers in your area by offering a service that's not commonly available, such as engine compartment cleaning. Just be sure you know what you're getting into if that's your choice. With all the electronic equipment packed under the hood these days, engine cleaning isn't easy, particularly if you have large hands that can't easily slip between the hoses and hardware. But the scratches and scrapes will be worth it if adding this kind of service will bring more customers to your door or more calls for your mobile service.

Detailers who have been in the business a while recommend keeping your detailing menu simple. Offering choices like a full interior/exterior detail, an interior-only detail, a wash and exterior-only detail, and maybe express services like waxing alone or carpet cleaning alone are more than enough options when you start out. Because not all services (like claying) are familiar to customers, you should create a service menu brochure that gives the components of each package and explains the more mysterious services. The brochure also can be used as a direct-mail piece and to upsell your services. Simply hand one to your customer when you take his/her keys and mention the full range of services you offer. You also should be sure to display a quantity of these service brochures in a plastic holder on your service counter or give one to mobile customers at the same time you give them a receipt. You'll find information about creating and printing a brochure in Chapter 10, but in the meantime, you can check out the sample brochure on page 14.

To help you make sure you're covering all your bases when you're detailing a car, use the Detailing Checklist on page 15.

Pricing Your Services

Setting appropriate prices for the work you do is always a difficult task for a new business owner. Price your services too high, and you'll limit the number of people who can afford them; price them too low, and you'll limit your profit potential and possibly give your customers the perception that you're not as professional or competent as the guy (or gal) down the street.

"Selling by price alone will put a detailer out of business because there is always someone who will sell cheaper," warns detailing industry expert R. L. "Bud" Abraham, who is also owner of Detail Plus Car Appearance Systems in Portland, Oregon. "As a rule of thumb, a detail shop should have a profit margin of at least 20 percent after all expenses, the detailer's salary, and benefits."

To illustrate how that would work, let's say it takes you three hours to do a full exterior detailing.

Beware!

Another good reason not to undercharge for services, even if you have a low break-even point, is that you'll be so booked up you won't be able to fit in any new customers. You need to have a steady stream of new customers to keep the business growing.

Sample Brochure

1. Cover

Great Lakes Automotive Detailing

The automotive reconditioning and restoration experts

(555) 555-0000

2. Back

Your vehicle can look like new again!

We know you take pride in your car, SUV, van, or truck. But Michigan weather can really take a toll on your prized wheels. So let the automotive experts at Great Lakes Automotive Detailing restore the showroom shine with a professional interior and exterior detailing.

Besides making your vehicle look great, detailing also is a wise investment. It can prolong the life and beauty of your vehicle. It can increase the value of a vehicle you're planning to sell. It even can minimize end-of-lease charges you might incur when you turn in your leased vehicle.

Trust the experts at Great Lakes Automotive Detailing

The pros at Great Lakes Automotive Detailing will maintain, recondition, and restore your vehicle using professional-grade equipment and high-quality products. To make your vehicle shine like new again, call today for an appointment.

(555) 555-0000

Great Lakes Automotive Detailing
5555 Jefferson Avenue
St. Clair Shores, Michigan 48051

(555) 555-0000

www.greatlakesdetailing.com
info@greatlakesdetailing.com

3. Inside

Detailing Services

- ⊛ Hand wash and dry, buff, and wax—$39.95
- ⊛ Interior vacuuming, plastic and vinyl/leather cleaning, conditioning—$29.95
- ⊛ Carpet/mat steam cleaning and conditioning—$39.95
- ⊛ Scotchguarding (upholstery, carpeting)—$29.95
- ⊛ Engine cleaning (grease removed, engine compartment cleaned)—$49.95
- ⊛ Odor removal—$35
- ⊛ Deodorizing—$25
- ⊛ Paintless dent repair—from $50
- ⊛ Paint touch-up, scratch repair—from $50
- ⊛ Vinyl/leather repair—from $25

Detailing Packages

Interior Detailing—From $100
- ⊛ Hand wash
- ⊛ Interior vacuum
- ⊛ Fabric seats, carpets, mats steam cleaned
- ⊛ Leather or vinyl seats cleaned and conditioned
- ⊛ Dash, console, trim, vents, pedals cleaned and protected
- ⊛ Windows cleaned
- ⊛ Doorjambs cleaned

Exterior Detailing—From $125
- ⊛ Hand washing and old wax removal
- ⊛ Clay bar dirt/grit removal
- ⊛ Buffing and waxing of painted surfaces
- ⊛ Tires dressed
- ⊛ Wheels polished, wheel wells protected
- ⊛ Windows and mirrors cleaned
- ⊛ Engine compartment cleaned

Note: All prices are approximate and may vary depending on the size and condition of the vehicle.

Deluxe Detailing—From $195
Your best value!

Includes all interior and exterior services listed at left, plus carpet and upholstery shampooing and Scotchguarding, engine cleaning and degreasing, and trunk and jamb cleaning.

Service hours
Monday-Friday
10 A.M. to 5 P.M.
Saturday
by appointment

Pickup and delivery service available with 24-hour notice. Visa, MasterCard, and American Express accepted.

Great Lakes Automotive Detailing
5555 Jefferson Avenue
St. Clair Shores, Michigan 48051

(555) 555-0000

www.greatlakesdetailing.com
info@greatlakesdetailing.com

Detailing Checklist

A detailing service includes cleaning and inspection of all the following areas:

Engine compartment
- ❑ Inside hood
- ❑ Engine and hoses
- ❑ Outer lip and water channel
- ❑ All painted surfaces

Exterior
- ❑ All painted surfaces polished
- ❑ All painted surfaces lusterized
- ❑ Vinyl or cloth top
- ❑ Front, side, and rear lights
- ❑ Front grill
- ❑ Front air dam
- ❑ Front and rear bumpers
- ❑ Doorjambs and hinges
- ❑ Gas tank compartment
- ❑ Wheel well edge and moldings
- ❑ Wheel well compartment
- ❑ Wheels
- ❑ Tires
- ❑ Rocker panels
- ❑ Chrome polished (door edges, bumpers, trim)
- ❑ Weather stripping
- ❑ Body side moldings
- ❑ Side mirrors
- ❑ License plate(s)
- ❑ Tailpipe
- ❑ Pinstripes (free from wax deposits)
- ❑ Windows (including edges)
- ❑ Window trim

Protective coatings applied to:
- ❑ Tires (tire dressing)
- ❑ Vinyl roof (vinyl dressing)

- ❑ Rubber bumpers, side moldings, weather stripping
- ❑ Dashboard
- ❑ Leather
- ❑ Wood trim
- ❑ Vinyl seats and door panels

Interior
- ❑ Floor mats
- ❑ Pedals, gearshift
- ❑ Headliner
- ❑ Dashboard
- ❑ Instrument panel (vents, knobs, gauges)
- ❑ Sun visors
- ❑ Interior mirrors
- ❑ Steering wheel
- ❑ Glove box, side storage boxes
- ❑ Center console
- ❑ Ashtrays (front and rear)
- ❑ Carpet/floor
- ❑ Seats
- ❑ Seat tracks
- ❑ Door panels
- ❑ Rear shelf
- ❑ All chrome/plastic trim
- ❑ Sunroof tracks
- ❑ Window trim
- ❑ Windows (including edges)

Trunk compartment
- ❑ Inside lid
- ❑ Interior carpet or vinyl
- ❑ Outer lip and water channel
- ❑ Place floor mats into trunk
- ❑ Replace items removed from vehicle

Comments:_____

Technicians: _____ Final inspection by: _____

Courtesy of Karen Duncan

Let's further assume that you want to make $30 an hour for the work, and your expenses (including soap, polishes, and the electricity to run your equipment) run $15 (a high estimate) on a regular-sized vehicle. Since your spouse is working, too, and already has the benefits covered, you don't pay for any through your business. So the formula to figure out a price for a full exterior detailing would be:

$$\$90 \ (\$30 \times 3 \text{ hours}) + \$15 = \$105.$$

Twenty percent of $105 is $21, so you should charge at least $126 for an exterior detailing. Since people tend to like nice round numbers, feel free to round that figure up to $130 or down to $125.

The same formula would work if you have employees, but of course you would pay them less per hour, so your profit would be higher. But if you decide to offer benefits, you'll have to figure in that amount, too. According to 2002 Bureau of Labor Statistics figures, benefits comprised 27.9 percent of total employee compensation. However, a more realistic figure for a small business like a detailer would be 10 percent. So if you're paying a technician $8 an hour for a 40-hour workweek, you also can expect to pay 10 percent of that person's $320 salary (or $32) for benefits like health insurance, paid vacation, and so on. Is that a good reason not to offer benefits? Maybe. But

The Price Is Right

The price you can charge for detailing services varies widely across the country, so here are some ranges for the most popular auto detailing services that you can refer to when you set your own prices:

○ Full detail: $150–$225 (or more for luxury vehicles)

○ Express detail: $40–$75

○ Hand wash and vacuum: $25–$40

○ Interior shampooing and cleaning: $80–$100

○ Machine polish and wax: $100–$150

○ Carpet dyeing: $75–$150

○ Black trim restoration: $25–$100

○ Paint touch-up: $75–$200

○ Paintless dent repair: $75–$150 per dent

○ Windshield repair: $25–$80

○ Window tinting: $100 and up

○ Leather and vinyl repair: $25–$75

not offering benefits can limit the number of people who want to work for you. It's something to think about when you get to the point that you need to hire help.

If you operate out of a fixed facility, you'll have to take into account operating expenses like your mortgage or lease and utilities when you set your prices. Chapter 13 talks about how to figure operating expenses and has an income and operating expenses worksheet you can use to help calculate your costs so you can adjust your price schedule as necessary. Just as a heads up: You can reasonably assume that your overhead will be from 40 to 50 percent of your labor and materials cost.

Need help calculating a reasonable hourly rate? Here's a simple formula. Let's assume you're a mobile detailer and you want to make $40,000 per year.

$$\$40,000 \div 52 \text{ weeks} = \$769 \text{ per week}$$

$$\$769 \div 48 \text{ (8 hours per day x 6 days per week)} = \$16 \text{ per hour}$$

$$\text{Add a 20 percent profit margin } (\$3.20) = \$19.20 \text{ per hour}$$

Then average in your supply costs, loan repayment, etc., and you'll have a good handle on how much you need to earn to make ends meet and put some money in the bank.

"A lot of detailers don't charge enough because they don't look at how much it costs to do business," says Karen Duncan of Union Park Appearance Care Center in Wilmington, Delaware, who also owned a detailing business called We Love Your Car for 15 years before a natural disaster put her out of business in 2003. "I put a lot of thought into my prices based on my expenses and how long it took to do the work. I ended up being higher priced than most detailers, but I had a good following and a good business," she says.

Other detailers don't charge enough because they quote prices over the phone without ever seeing the vehicle, according to Tom Schurmann, former owner of Masterfinish and current owner of Professional Detailing Systems in Lakewood, Colorado, who sold his detailing business after 32 years so he could try his hand at selling his detailing system to other detailers. "We never quoted or printed hard prices. I explained that to do the best job I had to see what the vehicle needed," Schurmann says. "If pushed, I would quote a ballpark spread, which seemed to make people want to stop by to see if they qualified for the low side. Some guys will go out on a limb and offer a $99 special over the phone, and then the customer turns up with a 15-passenger van that was in a field with cattle living in it."

Parts and Labor

Despite the fact that you'll have a finite number of tasks to perform as a detailer, you'll soon find out you'll have a lot of variety in your day-to-day business life. To begin with, you'll probably spend a fair amount of time on the telephone every day, booking appointments, ordering supplies, and talking to salespeople. If you're mobile, you'll also have to make up a work schedule so you know exactly where you're supposed to be at any given time of the day. If you have employees, you'll have to coordinate their schedules, referee when those schedules (or the employees themselves) collide, hold training sessions, hire new people to replace those who leave, visit high school career day events to troll for new prospects, and so on. You'll also have to deal with building and detailing equipment maintenance (including detailing your own equipment so it's a shining example of the good work you do). You'll be in charge

of money management, customer service, and the complaint department. Finally, it'll be your job to keep the work area clean, uncluttered, and swept up, and the bathrooms scrupulously clean.

Sounds like a lot for one person to do, doesn't it? Well, it is—and it's the reason why some detailers choose to hire an assistant manager to help with the chores. We'll talk more about personnel, including how to find qualified help, in Chapter 8. In the meantime, you'll need a weekly or monthly planner to help you keep appointments and activities straight and on schedule. You can pick one up at any office supply store. If you're computer-proficient, you might consider using a PC-based calendar or scheduler program instead. Microsoft Office, which is the industry standard in workplace software, gives you a calendar template in both Microsoft Word and Microsoft Publisher that you can use to note appointments and commitments, or you could try ScheduleEZ Pro (Software2020, $185). Unfortunately, there is no software on the market built specifically for the auto detailing industry, but we'll talk about other programs you can use to run your business in Chapter 6.

Tales from the (Store)Front

Whether you're going mobile or facility-based, you should make a decision about your hours of operation early on. Mobile detailers generally work during regular business hours because many of them do their stuff in the parking lots of office buildings while their customers are at work. Having Saturday hours may also be a good idea if you have clients who prefer a house call. In addition, if the weather foils your detailing schedule during the week, you can pick up the slack on the weekend. Standard business hours of 9 to 5 should be fine given the clientele you're likely to have, but of course when the days are longer, there's no reason why you can't detail in the evening if you're so inclined. Just pick your locations carefully—no matter how safe an area is, it's not a good idea to be out in the middle of nowhere with no one around late at night, especially when your attention is on your work and not the area around you.

The ideal place to do your mobile magic is in a temporary location, the way Anthony Orosco does. The owner of Ultimate Reflections in San Antonio has an arrangement with administrators at two hospitals to detail cars right on site. In both cases, the arrangements were made after cardiologists at the health-care facilities asked him to detail their cars at the hospital, and he doesn't pay anything for the use of the spaces, which are under cover. He simply washes and waxes the hospital security vehicles on a regular basis in exchange for permission to detail physicians' cars on site.

> **Tip...**
>
> ## Smart Tip
> Put the finishing touch on a professional detail job with a complimentary license plate touch-up. Use touch-up paint that matches your state's license plate color, then seal it with clearcoat spray. It only takes about ten minutes, and the customer will definitely be impressed with your extra effort.

Site-based detailers are more likely to have standard retail business hours of 10 A.M. to 6 P.M., six days a week. Because customers are accustomed to the late hours auto dealerships keep a couple of nights a week, you might consider staying open, too, particularly if your business is located near them. You may be able to attract some used-car prep work.

But Tom Schurmann of Professional Detailing Systems in Lakewood, Colorado, a detailer for 32 years, says that's not always the best way to go. When he first started his business, he did a lot of dealer work on what he calls the "burnout schedule," or, daily from 8 A.M. to 6 P.M. and Saturdays from 8:30 A.M. to 5 P.M. After a dozen years, his retail business was strong enough that he could start dropping the dealership work, which he said didn't pay as much as retail work anyway. Eventually, he dropped dealership work altogether.

"[Retail] only was the most relaxed schedule—8 to 5 and Saturdays by appointment," Schurmann says. "Instead of detailing 17 or more cars a day, we went down to three cars a day. And we ended up making more money doing less. It was a wonderful, enjoyable time."

Padding with Product

How would you like to make extra money each month with very little effort? Then plan to offer a carefully selected assortment of consumer detailing products.

According to merchandising experts, retail products can make your profits grow significantly with minimal effort. All you have to do is buy extra products from your supplier—like polishes and waxes, shampoos and chamois—mark them up for retail sale, and display them on shelving in your waiting area (preferably behind the counter where they can't walk away when your attention is elsewhere). Then remember to suggest certain products to your customers as they're cashing out. (This also works for mobile detailers, of course—you just keep a supply in your vehicle.) A smooth sales pitch might go something like this: "If you want to preserve that nice shine on your dashboard between detailings, you can use XYZ Product, which is what I just used. I've got it in stock for just $3.95 for a six-month supply."

Card 'Em

Need one more idea for add-on sales? Then try gift certificates or gift cards, which have become a hot commodity in the retail sales world. In addition to businesses like department, book, and grocery stores and service providers like hair salons, carwashes have been selling gift certificates successfully over the past few years, and they can work for you, too.

Gift certificates are great because they can bring in a lot of cash for a very small investment. The downside is, they're probably going to be redeemed at some point, which technically means you'll be providing services for nothing at that time. For that reason, you might want to tuck away your gift certificate cash in a separate account that you can draw against whenever a certificate is redeemed.

To launch your gift certificate program, purchase gift certificate software and paper (a few sources for them are listed in the Appendix), and simply include information about the availability of the certificates in your brochure and other advertising. Alternatively, you can invest in the type of electronic gift card systems that make up those plastic cards that look like credit cards, but frankly, that's a little expensive for a start-up business that probably won't sell many in the early days. However, we have included contact information for a few companies that sell electronic systems in case you're interested.

"We found that gift certificates were very lucrative," Schurmann says. "It was money upfront, and most recipients had never had a detail before. With our quality work, we gained a new customer for life. We also found it very easy to point out and sell upgraded packages to get them into our six-month return program."

Weather Beaters

As the saying goes, into every life a little rain must fall—but inclement weather can be a business buster for the detailer. The minute the forecast calls for rain, snow, ice, or even high winds that can kick up dust devils, the cancellations will pour in because no one is going to spend big bucks on a detailing that would be ruined the minute they drive out of your shop.

Mobile detailers know better than anyone that business grinds to a halt on bad-weather days. It's possible to erect a canopy over your work area and the vehicle you're pampering during a sudden downpour, but such a tent isn't meant for anything other than temporary shelter. So you have no recourse except to shut down for the day . . . or the week.

Mobile detailers like Anthony Orosco use their downtime to catch up on paperwork, order supplies, and read e-mail. But there are other money-making operations you can undertake to make the time off more profitable. For instance, some detailers expand into the electronic accessories installation market to beef up sales. Having a steady stream of alarm, keyless entry, audio system, remote starter, and neon license plate customers helps to off-

Bright Idea

A way to build goodwill in the community is by donating professional services (like an exterior detailing) or a bucketful of detailing products to charitable organizations for a fund-raiser or raffle. Just be sure you can afford the gift in terms of time and cost.

set weather downtimes. Of course, these service also decrease the amount of time you can spend detailing, so be sure not to take on more than you can handle.

Detailers like Mike Myers of Gem Auto Appearance Center in Waldorf, Maryland, have diversified as a way to stay busy. Myers went from a mobile operation to a fixed-location to aircraft and boat detailing. "With the weather here in the East, you could struggle in the winter months. I've had years when I wasn't fit to talk to. I'd get home and my wife would slide my food under the door. I ate a lot of pancakes," he says, laughing.

Prentice St. Clair, a San Diego detailing industry expert and owner of Detail in Progress, recommended in an issue of *Professional Carwashing & Detailing* magazine that establishing yourself as an expert who can recondition all types of surfaces is a great way to get add-on business that can carry you through downtimes. "You can create a poster for your shop and do a special mailing once a year titled, 'Did you know that we can . . .,' followed by a list of special cleaning situations you can handle with the chemicals and equipment you already have," St. Clair says. "These appointments could easily be set up after hours, on typically slow days, or during inclement weather."

Among the ways you can use your knowledge of detailing chemicals and equipment are to restore lawn and patio furniture, to pressure-wash vinyl siding, to remove stains from driveways and sidewalks, and to polish and wax garage floors.

Inclement weather is bad enough, but there's another type of weather condition that can have a devastating effect on a detailer's business. Drought conditions that result in water restrictions can effectively close down a detailing business—perhaps for good—because the owner must abide by the same restrictions as the rest of the community. And don't expect anyone except perhaps your most loyal customers to wait for you until the drought breaks. They're more likely to head for the nearest carwash, since carwashes usually are not required to curtail their water usage during a drought. There's nothing much you can do during a drought except pray for rain and look for some other work, including the add-ons mentioned earlier. Better yet, establish a relationship with a carwash to provide detailing services, as discussed in Chapter 1, so you'll have work to carry you through the dry spells.

Taking Care of Business
Your Guide to Market Research

If one day you decided that your tolerance for snowstorms and Arctic temperatures was way past its expiration date and a warmer climate was essential for ongoing good mental health, would you just call up a real estate broker and tell her to pick out a charming little bungalow for you in the tropical paradise of her choice? Probably not. You're more likely to take a more organized approach to house hunting, including specifying the type and size of abode you need and taking into consideration practical matters like proximity to schools and shopping and the availability of enough fast-food joints to keep your kids happy until they can vote.

This is the same kind of informed decision-making process you must use when you're considering where to set up shop for your detailing business (even if your "shop" is a mobile rig). You absolutely must scout out your target market to determine whether there's even a need for your services, as well as the likelihood that someone will be willing and able to pay for them. And the way to cue yourself in on that essential data is by conducting some market research.

The term "market research" may conjure up in your mind visions of bespectacled guys with clipboards interrupting family dinnertime from coast to coast. But in reality, there's way more to market research than just telemarketers and Nielsen ratings. It involves tasks like identifying and understanding the needs of promising market segments (a fancy term for customers), and differentiating your services from those of your competition. In short, it's a crucial part of the successful launch of a new business. So here's a crash course on how to make short work of basic market research so you can get down to doing the work you like best—detailing really cool cars (and maybe even some clunkers) and making trunkfuls of money.

Warning! Warning!

We interrupt this chapter to bring you a public service announcement that is crucial to the health of your business, both in its infancy and its old age: You must not bypass market research if you're serious about success. Now, we understand that you'll be tempted to rush out and buy an extractor, chamois, and buffing compound and start putting that spit shine on vehicles in need of pampering. But you cannot make money if you're marketing to the wrong audience, no matter how enthusiastic you are or how many car toys you have.

Market research will help you

- identify the people who are most likely to want and need your services.
- determine whether the place where you want to open for business can actually sustain the business.

- discover useful information that can help you avoid big problems down the road that could curtail or close your business.

Luckily, you can do your own market research armed with just a few simple tools, and it doesn't have to cost you an arm and a leg.

Rev It Up

The first thing you need to determine is the specific characteristics that influence the buying habits of your adoring public. These characteristics, known as demographics, will help you figure out how to position your service best. Here's an example: Let's say you've decided to work out of an actual facility because it will maximize your business tax deductions while giving you a place to store all your detailing stuff. You find a place you love—an inexpensive one-bay unit near an auto mall in a Big Ten college town with 100,000 people (a large percentage of whom are students). On the outskirts of Universityville are a number of middle-class "bedroom communities" with 1920s Craftsman-style bungalows. The area is hip, trendy, and peopled by young families with one wage earner and no day-care expenses.

The question is, Can your detailing business survive there? Let's decide by taking a look at the Demographic Analysis chart (see page 26) of this hypothetical geographical area.

Doesn't sound like a very good place to do business, does it? But then again, you might be surprised—just consider those auto dealerships that would be your neighbors in the auto mall. You might be able to flash your winning smile at the general managers of the dealerships and charm them into allowing you to detail their new or used cars.

So we can add one more demographic to the above list: Business owners who have automotive-related businesses. They have characteristics positively related to the occupation, income, and geographical location categories that are relevant to your business. So you might indeed be successful there, assuming you make all the right business moves to court the dealerships' business. If you can also devise a way to appeal to several demographic segments at one time (like dealers and the college students who actually have their cars on campus and might be good for a wash and wax from time to time), then your chances of business success are even better.

Dollar Stretcher

Be sure to check out the U.S. Census Bureau's web site at www.census.gov when you start your market research. This site has a wealth of demographic information organized by state and county that can be very useful when investigating the demographics of your target market. The information can be instantly downloaded at no charge.

So who is likely to be your best customer, besides those auto dealers? Probably baby boomers, who love having nice cars but don't have the time to care for them. Auto enthusiasts who garage their prized rides during inclement weather and would swoon at the sight of a swirl mark. Classic car collectors who show their vehicles in parades. People who want to spiff up their vehicles before trading them or turning them in at the end of a lease. And the list goes on.

Out of the demographics discussed above, one of the most significant to consider is the income levels of the people in the area in which you wish to do business. Just think back to the preceding example. We've already determined that you may have a hard time making a go of it in a town that has a lot of unemployed students. So before setting up shop, investigate the average income levels in your neighborhood. Look at data like the percentage of people who are employed full time and the types of jobs they hold. If there are a lot of blue-collar people in manufacturing or heavy industry jobs, a downturn in the economy could make cash tight and adversely affect your ability to keep customers. So could a plant shutdown or a scaling back of local services. Information like this is readily available through your local chamber of commerce or your city's economic development office, so take advantage of it and use it.

You'll also want to ask about the area's percentage of white-collar jobs and the types of companies that support them. You should probably avoid an area where the local economy is heavily supported by just one industry, like high-tech equipment manufacturing or mining for meteorites. An economic downturn can be devastating to the local economy, which in turn could take your business down with it as people spend their unemployment checks on food and prescription drugs instead of paintless dent repair or interior detailing.

Demographic Analysis

Age	Many of the inhabitants are young.
Education	Many have at least some college education.
Gender	There are probably more female than male students (the Census Bureau says 55 percent of college students are female).
Occupation	There is probably a fairly high unemployment rate (due to students and stay-at-home moms who don't work).
Income	It's probably low—either because they're in school or raising families on one income.
Geographical location	They live in an area where college football and partying are probably the main pastimes.

Finally, you'll want to look at overall population since a detailing business relies on volume and repeat business. A city with a high-density business district is going to be a better choice for the business than a rural community with one gas station and a post office. The Census Bureau and the local chamber of commerce are good sources of population data.

Conducting Market Research

This isn't as hard as you might think. To begin with, there are two types of research: primary research, which is gathered firsthand from people in response to written or verbal questions, and secondary research, which is collected by studying information gathered by other people. Both are helpful for detailers like you who are trying to build a business strategy.

There are three types of primary research that are useful for detailers.

1. *Historical.* Studying past data to understand your market (like checking business records to find out the failure rate for automotive businesses and detailers in general in your market).

2. *Observational.* Watching your potential customers to determine their buying behavior (such as camping out near an established detailer to observe what types of people—i.e., age, gender, etc.—use the business). Tom Schurmann of Lakewood, Colorado, used this method before opening his first shop, Masterfinish, in 1979. He studied the market for months. He took pictures of competitors' shops and then went into those shops and asked for quotes. He also recorded his experiences and observations about the location and its appearance, attitude, cleanliness, professionalism, and so on. Then he carefully reviewed his findings and determined that he would do a better job . . . and a new detailer was born.

3. *Survey.* Asking prospects what they're looking for in a detailer through the use of direct-mail pieces, telemarketing, and personal interviews. Of the three, direct-mail surveys are the most cost-effective and least time-consuming tool for gathering information for a new business owner on a small budget. Plus, they're relatively inexpensive to produce.

Direct-mail questionnaires can be a little tricky to write. You'll want to make sure your

> **Tip...**
>
> **Smart Tip**
> When doing a market survey, be sure your test panel is large enough to yield a statistically significant sample. According to industry experts, direct-mail response rates average just 10 percent, which would mean only 30 are returned out of 300. To obtain enough useful data, make your test panel as large as your budget will allow.

questions are short and to the point. They should mostly be open-ended, which means they can't be answered with just a "yes" or "no." For example, a simple question like "Would you be interested in mobile detailing done right at your home or office?" isn't very useful because if a respondent says "No," you haven't learned anything; you don't know the reasons behind the answer. A better question might be "How many times last year did you have your vehicle detailed?" Then follow up with questions like "If never, why not?" and "Which services did you like best?"

If you need help phrasing your questions for maximum impact, try getting help from the business school at your local university. According to David Williams, Ph.D., a professor in the marketing department in the School of Business at Wayne State University in Detroit, a marketing professor might be willing to draft your questionnaire for $500 to $1,000, which is a bargain compared to what a marketing firm would charge. Alternatively, he or she may assign your questionnaire as a class project and pass along the results to you free of charge.

If you'd like to try creating your own survey, check out the market research questionnaire postcard, which you can use as a guideline, on pages 29 and 30. You might insert this survey postcard in a direct mailing to prospective customers, complete with a market research letter like the one on page 31.

Shift into Gear

Once your questionnaire has been developed, the next step is to mail it out to a random sampling of consumers in your area. There are a number of companies and organizations that sell their mailing list to business owners like you for a nominal fee. These lists are usually organized in categories by demographics, so you can pick, for instance, heads of household aged 45 and up or couples with combined annual incomes of more than $75,000. Local homeowners' associations, list brokers, and even daily newspapers in major metropolitan areas are all good sources of mailing lists, as are the corporate offices of trade show companies, which often compile the names of attendees for their exhibitors.

Other places to look for mailing lists include the *Standard Rate and Data Service* directory, published by VNU, or the *Directory of Associations* (Gale Research), both of which are found in many large libraries and list publications and associations, respectively, that sell their lists. In addition, Karen Duncan of Union Park Appearance Care Center in Wilmington, Delaware,

Smart Tip
The best type of list to rent for direct mailings is the hot list, which consists of contact information for known buyers. These lists are usually compiled from magazine subscription lists, mail order buyer lists, and so on, and because the information is so fresh and accurate, they're usually more expensive to rent than lists compiled from books like the telephone directory.

Market Research Questionnaire Postcard

— Front of Postcard —

From:

_____

_____

_____

↑ **Important!** Be sure to fill this out.

NO POSTAGE
NECESSARY
IF MAILED
IN THE
UNITED STATES

BUSINESS REPLY MAIL

FIRST-CLASS MAIL   PERMIT NO. 5555   CHICAGO, IL

POSTAGE WILL BE PAID BY ADDRESSEE

ATTN: **Daniel Wayne**
Great Lakes Automotive Detailing
5555 Jefferson Ave.
St. Clair Shores, MI 48051

Fold Here

The automotive reconditioning and restoration experts

Tape Together Here

Market Research Questionnaire Postcard, continued

Back of Postcard

Please answer the following questions and return this postage-paid card for a chance to win a complete detailing package valued at $185.

1. What kind of vehicle do you drive?
   _____
   _____

2. Have you ever had it professionally detailed?
   ❑ Yes
   ❑ No

   If no, skip to question 6.
   If yes, how often do you have it detailed?
   ❑ Weekly
   ❑ Monthly
   ❑ Other (specify)_____
   _____

3. How much do you pay for interior/exterior detailing? _____
   _____

4. Would you prefer mobile detailing to dropping your vehicle off at a detailing shop?
   ❑ Yes
   ❑ No

5. Which detailing service is most important to you?
   ❑ Hand wash and vacuum
   ❑ Hand wax
   ❑ Upholstery cleaning
   ❑ Carpet dyeing
   ❑ Odor removal
   ❑ Windshield repair
   ❑ Paintless dent repair
   ❑ Other (specify) _____

6. What is the most you'd spend for a complete detail?
   ❑ $125   ❑ $150
   ❑ more than $150

7. Which of the following are important to you when it comes to using a detailing shop? (Check all that apply.)
   ❑ Price
   ❑ Extended business hours
   ❑ Detailers' training
   ❑ Ability to drop off without an appointment
   ❑ Quick service time
   ❑ Wide selection of retail products

8. What is your age?
   ❑ 18–29 ❑ 30–45 ❑ 46–60
   ❑ 61 and up

9. What is your household income?
   ❑ Under $25,000
   ❑ $25,000–$40,000
   ❑ $40,001–$55,000
   ❑ $55,001–$70,000
   ❑ $70,001 and up

10. What is your profession?
    _____

11. Please provide your e-mail address to receive information about detailing specials:
    _____
    _____

Market Research Letter

July 19, 2004

Mr. Greg Jakub
5555 Allard
Grosse Pointe Woods, Michigan 48236

Dear Mr. Jakub:

Please accept as our gift the enclosed $10 gift certificate toward any service valued at $100 or more at the new Great Lakes Automotive Detailing, opening in St. Clair Shores on September 1.

At Great Lakes, we specialize in providing professional interior and exterior detailing for everything from luxury vehicles to family sedans. In addition to hand washing and waxing your vehicle, we'll make the interior look like new. We also offer engine cleaning, paintless dent repair, and odor removal, all of which can restore your vehicle to showroom condition.

We hope you'll take a moment to fill out the brief questionnaire we've enclosed so we can determine how we can serve you best. If you'll return the enclosed postage-paid card with your responses, your name will be entered in a drawing for a complete detailing package valued at $185.

We look forward to serving you soon.

Very truly yours,

Daniel Wayne

Daniel Wayne
Owner
Great Lakes Automotive Detailing

5555 Jefferson Ave. · St. Clair Shores, Michigan 48051 · (555) 555-0000
www.greatlakesdetailing.com · info@greatlakesdetailing.com

had good luck drumming up new business using a real estate broker customer list that she obtained through her county government.

Lists are usually rented to you for one-time use at a flat rate of anywhere from $40 to $100 per 1,000 names. You can usually get the lists on either pressure-sensitive labels or disk. Because the minimum number of records you can buy is usually 1,000, you can do your own random sampling by removing every *nth* label (as in 4th or 10th) or delete records from the disk until you get the number you want.

Surveys don't have to be fancy, but they do have to be neat, spelled correctly, and professional looking. To save money, you can design the survey on your home computer (make sure it's clean and uncluttered). Then stop by a quick-print shop like Kinko's and have it photocopied on quality paper. You'll pay only about 8 cents per copy. (Office Max, for example, has a great online printing service—you tell them how many copies, what color paper you want, etc., then you attach your document, and the job will be ready for you at the store you designate.)

Gun It

If you're on a tight budget, you may have to rely more heavily on secondary research. Thanks to the internet, you may not have to spend a dime of your start-up money on research. You just need to know where to look to find information that will help you make general marketing assumptions. So start with local utility companies, which may even share their demographic info free of charge; local economic development organizations; your local municipality (city, county, parish, etc.), which keep census tracts on file that include information about population density and distribution; and your friendly Uncle Sam, who collects data on just about anything you can

---

Guerrilla Marketing

Dave Echnoz of 14/69 Carwash Supercenter in Fort Wayne, Indiana, developed a surefire way to pick up new dealership business—he asked for it. Once a week, he'd drive to all the car lots in the area and note which new and used cars needed detailing. Then on Monday morning, he'd call the dealership managers and make a specific pitch, like "There's a blue Ford on your lot that needs work. I can come by and pick it up, and have it ready for you today."

This approach worked like a charm for both new and used vehicles. "Dealerships like that aggressive nature," Echnoz says. "And when I'd get there with the car, I'd offer to take another one back with me."

think of. The only problem with federal data is that it's not always fresh—it's often a year or two old since the wheels of the government grind slowly—but it still may be useful (and since it's usually free, the price is right). Sources that might be of help include the granddaddy of information gathering, the U.S. Census Bureau (www.census.gov), as well as the SBA (www.sba.gov).

Once you start looking, you'll find that everyone has statistics they'll share. Not the least of these are your local library, chamber of commerce, trade publications (like *Modern Car Care*), and industry associations. There isn't a detailing trade association, but you can try one of the carwash organizations in the Appendix. Finally, the Yellow Pages can be a useful source. The "Auto Detailing" listings can help you determine at a glance just how many legitimate detailers are already operating in your area and where they're located.

Map Your Course

So now you're on track to understanding your market. Next up is the process of understanding yourself and your purpose, both of which help your business head in the right direction—right toward profitability and success. An effective way to do this is by writing a mission statement just like the big corporations do.

Even if you've never been to business school, you probably already have an insight into the process of a strong mission statement. Remember the scene in the 1996 movie *Jerry Maguire*, when the title character, played by Tom Cruise, writes a description of everything that's wrong about being a sports agent and gives "a suggestion for the future of our company"? Basically, what he wrote was a mission statement, although at 30 pages it was more like a mission *novel*.

Unlike Jerry's leviathan document, your mission statement should be a brief statement that describes your company's purpose and goals. A one- or two-sentence mission statement that covers what the company does, who it does it for, and why it does it can cover all the bases adequately.

A simple mission statement for a detailer might say this: "Great Lakes Auto Detailing will cater to the car-care needs of busy professionals and classic car owners by providing complete detailing and paintless dent repair services from a centrally located facility. The goal is to have an active client base of 100 people in the first six months."

Here's another possible approach: "Great Lakes Auto Detailing is a full-service car-care business that uses professional-grade equipment

Fun Fact

In the movie *Jerry Maguire*, the title character is fired after talking incessantly about his mission statement. But all's well that ends well: It ultimately did put him on the right track to personal success in his own business. Plus, he got the girl at the end. What more could you ask for?

▲

as a way to exceed the quality of service provided by its three nearest competitors. This level of professionalism, plus my skill and attention to detail, will lead to first-year sales of $60,000."

And here are a couple of actual mission statements provided by detailers *Entrepreneur* spoke to:

> "To provide exceptional value and customer care to the motoring public by maintaining the beauty of their vehicles."
>
> *—Detail in Progress, San Diego*

> "The purpose of Gem Auto is to provide the general public with a service by which they can restore, enhance and/or maintain the appearance of the interior and exterior of their vehicle. We remain convenient to everyone in our market area and offer services that stay within the affordability of any car owner."
>
> *—Gem Auto Appearance Center, Waldorf, Maryland*

As you can see, mission statements can be of varying lengths (the classic is Pepsi's two-word mission statement: "Beat Coke"), but the length isn't as important as what it means to you. For this reason, it's a good idea to review your mission statement regularly to make sure your business is moving toward achieving its goals. For example, if you notice in your fifth month of operation that your year-to-date revenues are only $24,000 when you expected them to be at $30,000 in six months, you'll need to make some moves (like advertising more or sending reminders to past customers) to pick up the extra $6,000 needed to meet your goal. At $185 for a complete detail, you'd have to detail 33 vehicles to meet that goal, which might not be possible in just a month. If you had reviewed your mission statement earlier, you would have been able to spread those 33 vehicles out over more time.

On page 35 you'll find a worksheet that you can use to help you with the process of creating the right mission statement for your business—and keep you from writing a *Jerry Maguire*-style epic.

Mission Statement Worksheet

Here's your chance to try your hand at writing your own mission statement. Start out by answering the following questions:

1. Why do you want to start an auto detailing business? _____

_____

_____

_____

2. What skills do you bring to the business? (Include education and detailing skills.) _____

_____

_____

3. What is your vision for success? Where do you think you'll be in one, two, and five years? _____

_____

_____

4. Which services do you want to offer? _____

_____

_____

5. Which customers do you want to service? (Be specific—e.g., general public, auto dealerships.) _____

_____

_____

Using this information, write your mission statement here:

Mission Statement For
(your business name)

_____

_____

_____

_____

_____

_____

_____

_____

Throttling Up
for Success

By now you should have a good idea whether there are enough gearheads, auto enthusiasts, and car collectors in your target market to keep your business revved up. But before you can fire up the extractor and get down to business, you need to build your own reliable business chassis from the ground up. And that means addressing the standard equipment that comes

Start-Up Checklist

Here is a list of things you need to do before launching your business:

❑ Select a business name and apply for a dba.

❑ Investigate legal business forms or consult with an attorney for advice.

❑ Apply for a federal employer identification number (only if you're forming a corporation or partnership).

❑ Check local zoning regulations for restrictions on homebased businesses, if applicable.

❑ Apply to your municipality for a business license.

❑ Write a business plan.

❑ Write a marketing plan.

❑ Consult with an accountant regarding financial and tax considerations for establishing and operating a business.

along with the joy of owning your own business: namely, legalities like picking the appropriate business form, selecting a name, and insuring the whole operation against liability and loss.

Business Structure

Among the very first things you should do is to select the legal form under which you'll operate. This is important for two reasons. First, since the IRS is going to be very interested in anything you do that makes money, you'll want to pick the type of business that has the best tax advantages for your particular situation. Second, each type of legal structure has certain benefits and disadvantages when it comes to owner liability. You need to choose carefully to protect yourself and your livelihood.

In general, auto detailing businesses operate as one of four basic legal entities: sole proprietorship, partnership, corporation, or limited liability company (LLC).

Sole Proprietorship

Out of the four common legal forms, the sole proprietorship is the easiest to form. In fact, all you have to do is select a business name, file some simple paperwork at the county or state level to establish a fictitious business name of your choice, obtain a business license in the municipality in which you'll operate, and open a business checking account in the business's new name. In general, you don't have to establish credit in your business's name; rather, you can whip out your personal plastic to charge business purchases like office equipment or professional detailing products. This can vary by supplier, however. Check with the companies you do business with to determine whether it's necessary to establish a business account.

As a sole proprietor, you'll get tax benefits like business expense deductions even though you don't have to file a separate business tax return. Instead, business income and expenses are reported on Schedule C of your personal IRS Form 1040 tax return, and your profits are taxed as ordinary income. You will, however, pay an extra self-employment tax, which essentially is the other half of the Social Security tax that you have to pay because you're the employer of record.

> **Smart Tip**
>
> If you operate your business under your own name, you can use your Social Security number as your federal ID. But if you choose another name, or you form a partnership or corporation, you must have a federal employment identification number. To apply for one, file form SS-4 (available at any IRS office or at www.irs.ustreas.gov).

As the sole owner, you reap all the profits from the business (minus Uncle Sam's generous portion, of course), you manage it the way you want, and you're completely responsible for its actions. And therein lies the problem with sole proprietorships. As sole owner, you are personally liable for any losses, bankruptcy claims, or legal actions (like liability suits) that may be brought against your business. Any or all of these situations can quickly wipe out not only your business assets but also your personal assets, including savings accounts, stocks and bonds, vehicles, and even your house. That's a scary thought, particularly given the litigious society in which we live today. As a result, good liability coverage is a *must* in this business, no matter whether you're detailing 15-year-old Yugos or Rolls-Royces. You'll find a discussion of insurance options in Chapter 5.

> **Beware!**
>
> If you're planning to sell detailing products, you need a seller's permit, which enables you to buy products for resale without paying sales tax. The permit may be free of charge, but you may have to post a security deposit. Check with your state's board of equalization or department of revenue to find out the requirements.

Another disadvantage of sole proprietorships is that you're liable for employees who make mistakes while working for you. There's insurance available to manage this liability (which we'll talk about later), but it could end up being insufficient to cover claims. Then your personal property would again be at risk.

Finally, sole proprietors sometimes find it difficult to obtain financing for their fledgling venture. As you'll see later in the book, you can establish a new detailing business with a fairly low capital outlay, but if your business requirements exceed your bank account and/or your credit line, you may find that commercial lenders will be reluctant to fill your coffers with much-needed cash. Those that are willing to ante up are likely to insist on collateral, which again puts your personal assets at risk.

Partnership

Although many detailers start out in the business as independent operators, you might have a good buddy who would make a good business partner. So a partnership might be the way to go. If you're so inclined, you could also form a partnership with your spouse even if he/she isn't actively involved in the business. That way, if something happens to you, your spouse would take possession of the business. Compare that setup to a sole proprietorship, which is dissolved when the owner dies or declares bankruptcy, and you can see the wisdom of at least considering a partnership with your better half.

There are two types of partnerships—general and limited. In a general partnership, each partner participates in the day-to-day operation of the business, from servicing customers to wrestling with balance sheets. In a limited partnership, a general partner manages the business while the limited partner supplies working capital but doesn't actively participate in daily operations. Unless you have a rich relative or moneyed friends in really high places, you're probably more likely to form a general partnership.

Like sole proprietorships, partnerships are easy to establish. All you need is a verbal or written agreement between the partners, although a written partnership is definitely recommended. You'll also need to establish a business checking account on which both (or all) partners can draw.

Business profits are divvied up among the partners based on the percentage of the business each owns; these profits are then taxed as personal income on each person's individual tax return. You'll also have to file a few federal forms related to the partnership, which are discussed in IRS Publication 541, *Partnerships*. You can pick up a copy of the guide at your local IRS office, or you can download it for free from the IRS web site (www.irs.gov).

As you might expect, the main downside of a partnership is personal liability. Each partner is liable for the other's actions (like when your partner accidentally rolls a client's custom SUV after swerving to avoid an overturned kielbasa truck on the interstate). Each partner also assumes unlimited liability in the event the business is sued, which means that both personal and business assets would be at risk.

Because each partner is responsible for the actions of the other, a written agreement between partners is strongly recommended, even if you've known your prospective business partner for years or are related to him/her. This includes spouses, since a partnership is dissolved upon the death or bankruptcy of one of the partners unless the partnership agreement stipulates otherwise. Have an attorney with small-business experience draw up an agreement that spells out all the terms of the partnership, including responsibilities, rights, and percentage of business ownership. This protects the remaining partner and his/her interests if one of you decides to leave the business or you have to dissolve the partnership for any reason (divorce, bankruptcy, relocation, etc.). You'll find information about hiring an attorney in Chapter 5.

Corporation

If limiting your liability is high on your priority list (as it would be if you're planning to detail high-end or collectible vehicles), then establishing a corporation is a smart move. A corporation is considered to be an entity completely separate from the business owner and, as such, is responsible for its own debts and actions, including liability.

The most common type of corporation is the C corporation, which offers limited liability protection, tax benefits for the health and life insurance premiums you pay, and the ability to transfer ownership if you decide to change careers or retire to Aruba. But these benefits don't come cheap; business profits are taxed twice, first at the corporate tax rate, then again at the personal tax rate because the owner and all employees are considered employees of the corporation. That can take a big bite out of profits.

An S corporation may be a more attractive choice for a detailer. With an S corporation, only the owner pays personal taxes on the profits—the corporation isn't liable. This preserves more of the profits, but there are fewer tax deductions and more restrictions. For instance, you'll be required to file articles of incorporation, elect officers (relatives are A-OK), and hold an annual meeting. The good news is that an informal meeting with a written agenda held in a service bay amidst your buffers and clay bars will fulfill the annual meeting requirement. The other good news is that you'll probably find it easier to obtain any start-up financing you need if you're incorporated, although the lending institution still may require you to offer personal assets (a car, investments, or your home) as collateral.

When you're ready to establish your corporation, you may wish to consult an attorney to help you make the right decision on which type to choose. He or she also can handle the incorporation. However, the incorporation process isn't very complicated, so if you're adventurous you can do the job yourself. A do-it-yourself incorporation costs about $50 to $300 vs. $400 to $1,000 when handled by an attorney. There even are incorporation kits available from office supply stores that run as little as $29.95 (the names of a few companies that sell these kits are listed in the Appendix).

Smart Tip

Tip...

An S corporation or LLC may be the best choice for a detailing shop with one to five employees, while a C corporation may be more advantageous for a larger shop, according to detailing industry expert R. L. "Bud" Abraham. Consult your attorney and accountant for help choosing which one suits your situation best.

You'll also find additional tips and insight into the incorporation process on *Entrepreneur*'s web site at www.entrepreneur.com.

Limited Liability Company

Another common type of business entity is the limited liability company, or LLC. This type of business format has gained popularity recently because it combines the tax structure of a partnership yet protects the business owner from personal liability the way a corporation does. It's often compared to the S corporation because of its tax advantages. Your attorney can help you determine whether an LLC is the right legal form for your detailing business.

The Name of the Game

Now that you've decided on a business structure, you'll need to select a business name that suggests high performance and attention to detail while evoking the type of service you offer.

Here are the names of some detailing shops currently operating around the country:

- Angel's Detail Shop
- Attention to Detail
- Bear Essentials Auto Salon
- Big Poppa's Auto Detailing
- Canuck Cleaning Service
- Chief's Squeaky Clean
- Jolly Wolly Detail Shop
- Littleton Auto Detailing
- Khan Komplete Kar Kare Service
- Perfection Plus Auto Detailing
- Pristine Auto Detail
- Rick's Custom Detail Shop Inc.
- Sparkling Image Detail & Custom Work

Which ones appeal to you? Probably the ones that are clever or catchy. A lot of auto detailers choose creative names that channel auto themes (like Speedway Auto Laundry), possibly because ordinary names are too boring for America's car-crazy society. Or maybe it's because a lofty name pumps up the business's image the same way a V-12 turbocharges a hot car.

Be that as it may, when you're choosing a name, stay away from ones that are too over-the-top, like "Race to the Finish Auto Detailing" or "The Suds Stud." *Cute* doesn't work well in this industry, either (even if you're a woman—or rather, *especially* if you're a woman), because it tends to make you seem less professional. That, in turn, can undermine the confidence your clientele will have in you to get the job done well. Need some help selecting the perfect name? You'll find a worksheet you can use to brainstorm ideas on page 44. You can also check the Yellow Pages (both the real and the virtual versions) for idea starters.

By the way, even though clever names tend to be more memorable, that doesn't mean you shouldn't name your detailing business after yourself. A simple, business-like name consisting of your name and a business description (like Mitch's Auto Detailing) can make the business seem more credible and reliable. It's also beneficial because many people like dealing with the owner of the company. So unless you have a name people will find difficult to pronounce, like "Bill Przewodniczki," feel free to name your offspring after its mom or dad.

If you do decide to use your own name, you should open a business checking account immediately to make it easier to distinguish between business deposits/expenditures and personal transactions. The wisdom of doing so will become very clear to you at 11:59 P.M. on April 15, as you struggle to separate the legitimate business transactions from the receipts for day care, groceries, and so on.

Once you've selected the name, take it out for a test spin before you invest in any promotional materials or a Yellow Pages ad. Have a friend call you a few times so you can answer the phone using the new name. It should be easy to say (just imagine saying, "Phil Vandevere's Speedy Auto Detailing Shop" a few dozen times a day). Names heavy on alliteration ("Sunshine State Detail Shop") and those with words that are hard to distinguish over the phone ("Buck's Auto Express") also should be avoided.

Staking a Name Claim

Once you've settled on the perfect moniker for your business, it has to be registered—usually at the county, borough, or parish level—to ensure its uniqueness. This simple process is necessary because, in essence, you're establishing a fictitious identity (even if you use your own name in the company name) and only one company at a time can have the same name in your market area.

To register a new business name, you must file an "assumed name" or dba ("doing business as") statement. It will cost you $10 to $50 to register the name, which gives you the privilege of using the name for a limited period of time, usually three to five years. When the time expires, you simply renew the dba by paying another fee. If you keep anteing up, you basically can have the name forever. But before you get permission to operate under your dba, a search is done by the government entity that accepts your application to make sure the name isn't already in use. You might be able to do

Business Name Worksheet

Would you prefer not to use your own name in your business name but you're having some trouble selecting the perfect moniker? Try using this worksheet as an idea starter.

First, list the top three things that come to mind when you think of the word "detailing" (such as adjectives like "perfect" or "manicured," or nouns like "carpet"). Be creative!

1. _____
2. _____
3. _____

Next, list the top three things that come to mind when you think of the word "automobile."

1. _____
2. _____
3. _____

List three unique landmarks or other geographical references relevant to your city, state, or regional area that characterize the marketplace where you're located (like the St. Louis Arch or Times Square).

1. _____
2. _____
3. _____

Now, try combining elements from these three sections in different ways.

1. _____
2. _____
3. _____

Once you've come up with something you like, try putting it to the test:

❑ Say it aloud several times to make sure it's easily understood, both in person and over the phone. (Remember the name "The Suds Stud?" Besides being a terrible name, the "s" sounds make it difficult to pronounce, let alone understand on the phone.)

❑ Thumb through your local Yellow Pages directory to make sure someone else isn't already using the name you've chosen.

❑ Check with your county seat or other official registrar to make sure the name is available (since someone may have already claimed the name but may not be using it yet).

If your name passes these tests, then you're ready to officially register it.

the search yourself by logging on to the local government entity's web site and searching the online business registry. If you happen to choose a name that's already being used, you'll have to pick something else, so it's a good idea to come up with a couple of names when you do your initial brainstorming.

Vroooooom with a View

At this point in the business development process, it's likely you've already made some decisions about whether you're going to establish a mobile business, or intend to work out of your garage at home or in a commercial facility. If you're planning to detail cars in your driveway, you should be aware that there could be local ordinances that restrict or ban businesses from operating in residential areas. The idea, of course, is to protect homeowners from excessive traffic and noise, both of which you might generate with a homebased detailing business. For instance, the equipment you'll be using—vacuums, extractors, and buffers—tends to be loud, especially if it's running all day

That's My Name!

In addition to making sure no one else is using the business name you've selected at the local level, you should also do a wider search to make sure you're not infringing on someone else's name. Companies and even individuals get pretty upset about that.

There are many places you can search on the internet for name conflicts. Among them are:

❍ Your state's secretary of state or Department of Motor Vehicles office, which may have a searchable database of names against which you can compare your name

❍ The U.S. Patent and Trademark Office web site (www.uspto.gov)

❍ Business directories such as www.InfoSpace.com, www.InfoUSA.com, or www. bigyellow.com

❍ Popular internet portals like Yahoo! and Google (plug in your name and see what comes up)

❍ Network Solutions (www.networksolutions.com) and www.register.com, both of which can tell you whether your name is already being used as a domain name

Stat Fact
A thoroughly researched business plan is about 25 pages long and can take 300 hours to prepare (which includes doing the research, compiling financial information, conducting surveys, and writing). But detailer Tom Schurmann reports the effort is worth it—after he wowed the bank with his 40-page business plan, he got the financing he needed in one day.

long. If you offer pickup and delivery service, you could have several customers' vehicles parked at your home, which could be seen as a traffic hazard. And if you're a mobile detailer, you may have to park your rig in the street when you're not on the road detailing cars, where it could be viewed as an unsightly obstacle to smooth traffic flow. It's not likely you'll be allowed to erect a sign on your front lawn to drum up business.

So to avoid a lot of bureaucratic hassle, be sure to check with your local government office early in the process of establishing the business to see if homebased businesses are allowed. You may find you'll need special permits to operate as well as a business license. Such a license is usually quite inexpensive and is renewable annually. If, by chance, you're turned down for a license because of zoning restrictions, you can apply for (and possibly receive) a variance from the municipal planning commission. Plan to attend the commission's next meeting to show that your business won't disrupt the neighborhood. Having an extra-long driveway where you can park cars or installing sound deadening panels on the walls of your garage are measures you can take to help convince the municipal denizens that you'll be a good neighbor.

Business Details

Now that you've got all that corporate and legal stuff out of the way, you're well on your way to getting your business up and running. What you need now is a road map to guide your steps as you build a viable and profitable auto enterprise. That road map is your business plan.

Now everyone knows that men, in general, don't like to ask for directions or rely on maps to get them where they want to go. (That's not a biased statement—studies have shown that women generally are more willing to use a map or stop for directions.) But your business plan is one map you definitely shouldn't be without. It outlines your plans, goals, and strategies for making your business successful and, as such, should be referred to often. It keeps you on track by helping you manage your business in the most professional way possible. But it also should be adaptable so it can change to meet current challenges and opportunities in your market.

In addition to keeping your ride on the road, there's another good reason to have a carefully developed business plan. Banks and other financial institutions expect you to have one when you apply for financing for your business. Most of the time they won't even consider a credit application from a business that doesn't have a comprehensive business plan; your business plan demonstrates that you're serious about your detailing business and have developed a viable plan to make it successful.

Even if you self-finance your business, you need a detailed business plan. Even if you don't consider yourself a writer, you should be able to draw up your own viable plan. But if you need assistance, contact your local Small Business Development Center (found in the federal section of the Yellow Pages under the SBA or by logging on to www.sba.gov/sbdc), or check your local bookstore or library for one of the many books or software packages available that make writing a business plan a manageable task.

Smart Tip

Tip...

The SBA has a wealth of free publications that can be helpful to small businesses. Two to try: Publication MP 21, *Developing a Strategic Business Plan,* and Publication MP 31, *Handbook for Small Business.* They're both available at local SBA offices or by visiting www.sba.gov/library.

Under the Hood
Choosing a Professional Pit Crew

So far we've talked about structure of your detailing business and the mechanics of establishing it properly. Now it's time to consider the people you'll need on your team to keep the business humming along. Those professionals include an attorney, an accountant, and an insurance agent.

Now you might be thinking, "Hey, I'm just a little guy trying to make a living. I haven't even bought any Armor All yet, and you're telling me I need a bunch of high-priced consultants?"

Well, yes. Because no matter how large your detailing operation is—from a one-person mobile business to a business with employees and a fixed location—you need experienced business professionals who can help you avoid common start-up blunders and free you from the more mundane aspects of running the business, like preparing your corporate taxes and reading contracts. That also frees you up to spend your time on the activities you do best—like detailing cars, SUVs, and trucks. Having these pros on your management team will help make your business seem much more stable and solid, which won't escape the notice of bankers and suppliers you'll be approaching for financial assistance.

A Powerful Ally

Trial attorney Henry G. Miller once said, "The legal system is often a mystery, and we, its priests, preside over rituals baffling to everyday citizens." That pretty much sums up why you need an attorney on your business team.

A trustworthy, competent attorney is invaluable for sorting out the intricacies of the law, from negotiating leases and reading contracts to defending you against unfounded claims of detailing crimes committed on a Ford truck. He/she also can help you with tax planning and loan negotiations, as well as when you're signing a contract for a lot of money. Even the one-person detailer should have an attorney on standby for those unexpected things that tend to pop up when you're in business for yourself.

Believe it or not, it's possible to find an attorney whose fee schedule fits into your budget. To keep costs down, avoid large law firms, which tend to service larger clients with big corporate bankrolls, and opt instead for a one- or two-person practice. Even in a small firm, rates typically start at around $100 per hour, but the denizens of those smaller practices are more likely to be willing to work within your humble budget.

You'll probably find it most cost-effective to engage an attorney who charges a flat fee for routine work, such as writing letters or setting up a corporation, or one who offers a

Dollar Stretcher

A prepaid legal plan can be a great way to save money on attorney fees. You just pay a small annual fee to get services like telephone consultations, letter writing, and contract review provided by a qualified attorney. The plans also may provide legal representation at a reduced cost. You can find attorneys who provide such services in the phone directory under "Legal Service Plans."

business start-up package. Such packages usually include the initial consultation and all activities related to the incorporation process, including the filing of paperwork with your state and other corporate formalities. You can expect to pay around $900 for this service. Other common fee arrangements include paying an upfront retainer, out of which the attorney draws as work is completed, or paying via contingency, which means the attorney is paid a percentage of whatever is won in a lawsuit settlement.

To find an attorney who suits you, ask around. Other small-business owners are the best sources for recommendations as are organizations like the chamber of commerce or your local economic development group. Barring that, you can try an attorney referral service, which can be found in many counties around the country.

Money Managers

OK, so maybe you're not yet convinced that you need an attorney. But chances are, you can see the wisdom of hiring an accountant to handle your bookkeeping. Because unless you have a divinely inspired knack for transforming long columns of numbers and boxes of receipts into tidy (and accurate) spreadsheets and forms that will make Uncle Sam happy, you probably won't want to do your own accounting beyond loosely tracking credits and debits. For that purpose you can use a spreadsheet program like Microsoft Excel. For heavy-duty bookkeeping, you need an accountant.

Count on It

If you need an accountant but you don't have a lot of cash for the fees, consider using a public accountant rather than a CPA. Public accountants aren't state-licensed, so they generally charge less than CPAs. But they also can't represent you before the IRS if you're called in for an audit. CPAs, on the other hand, are college-educated and have to pass a rigorous state-administered certification examination. Most business experts recommend using only CPAs because their credentials are universally recognized and respected by bankers, investors, and others in the business world.

To keep tax preparation costs under control, look for an enrolled agent instead of an accountant. They're fully qualified to represent you before the IRS in case of an audit. Enrolled agents can be found in the Yellow Pages under "Accountants" or through the directory found on the National Association of Enrolled Agents' web site at www.naea.org.

Accountants are skilled at handling important tasks like creating profit and loss statements, making financial projections, forecasting cash flow, and setting up accounting systems—all of which are important to even the smallest business. In addition, an experienced accountant is invaluable for interpreting tax law, which is very complicated and changes frequently. (In fact, the IRS issues new tax rulings every two hours of every business day!)

For all this expertise, you can expect to pay an hourly rate that varies by type of practice, location, expertise, and education. For instance, according to the *New Hampshire Job Outlook and Locator*, the average hourly wage of an accountant with a Bachelor's degree is just over $21 while the PCPS *Management of an Accounting Practice Survey* indicated that a CPA in a small accounting firm would have a billing rate of $83 per hour.

Your attorney, banker or other business owners in the detailing or carwash industry are good sources of referrals. Alternatively, the American Institute of Certified Public Accountants' branch in your state can refer you to a qualified CPA, or you can find a professional accountant on the www.accountant-finder.com web site. It's preferable to select someone who has experience with small-business clients because they're more likely to be tuned into your tax and financial situation.

As mentioned earlier in this chapter, depending on your level of numerical aptitude and interest, you may be able to handle some of your own accounting tasks by using an accounting software package. In addition to crunching numbers accurately, these packages are useful for keeping financial records, writing checks to suppliers, and so on. Programs like QuickBooks also have a feature that allows you (or your accountant) to download financial records and other information entered into your worksheets directly to TurboTax business tax software, which is a great timesaver at tax time.

Managing Risk

Anyone who's ever owned a vehicle knows the necessity of having good car insurance. In this country, even clunkers have to be insured, even if it's only to protect the *other* guy against damage your decrepit battle cruiser might inflict in a collision.

The same theory applies to your new detailing business. You'll need coverage to protect yourself against a whole carload of what-ifs (hark back for a moment to what we said about liability in Chapter 4). To help you steer through the winding back roads of Insuranceville, you'll want to rely on the services of a professional insurance broker.

An insurance broker differs from an insurance agent because a broker represents may different insurance products from many different companies, while "regular" insurance agents are employed by a single company and sell only that company's products. Going with a broker is advantageous for two reasons. First, the broker won't be emotionally attached to any one company's products and therefore will be more willing to shop around. Second, by comparing many policies and levels of coverage against one another, a broker often can get you a good insurance policy at a rate you can afford.

To find a reputable business insurance broker, tap your business acquaintances or attorney for recommendations, or look in the "Business" subcategory of the "Insurance" listings in the phone directory for leads. It's best to select a broker who understands the concerns of small-business owners, especially those who need good liability insurance (a primary requirement for auto detailers like you). Ask to see a client list when you talk to a prospective broker to get a feel for the types of clients he/she services.

> ## Smart Tip Tip...
>
> A commonsense approach to risk management can help you avoid accidents in the shop or on a mobile job. For instance, don't let employees do work they're not qualified to perform, be sure to eliminate trip-and-fall hazards like piles of wet towels in the work area and ice in your parking lot, and make sure your ground fault interrupter outlets aren't overloaded.

One of the most important decisions you'll make when buying business insurance is determining exactly how much coverage you'll need, based on how much risk you're willing and financially able to take. That means if you're going to specialize in high-end vehicles like sports cars or classic cars, you'll need a liability policy with higher coverage than if you detail the family sedans of the world.

Not surprisingly, many detailers don't approach their business insurance needs this way. Instead, they're more concerned with cutting corners to control costs, and, as a

Go for Broke(r)

If you're considering buying or leasing a building for a detailing shop, you should consider consulting a professional real estate broker. A broker can be invaluable for helping you find the perfect location—especially in a tight real estate market—because he/she will know which commercial locations are available that would suit your needs, how dynamic the area you're considering is in terms of growth potential, and how much space goes for in the target area. He/she also can act as an intermediary with the seller or landlord and then help with negotiations when you're ready to sign on the dotted line. If you use a broker, be sure to find out up front who pays the broker's fee. Sometimes the seller pays the fee; other times, the seller and the buyer split the fee. If you're footing the bill, you'll be expected to sign a contract agreeing to pay for services rendered.

Beware!

To qualify for the self-employed health insurance deduction, the insurance plan must be established under your business name. The IRS says that the deduction may be allowed if you either paid the premiums yourself, or your partnership or S corporation paid them. The premium amounts also must be included in your gross income.

result, they're often underinsured—if they're insured at all. But the problem is that all it takes is one disaster—like having an inexperienced technician enthusiastically power-buff a classic car right down to the metal or hosting the first tornado to roar through your community in half a century—and your entire investment and livelihood could be wiped out.

"There seems to be a certain amount of resistance to insurance, especially among smaller operators," says Prentice St. Clair, a San Diego detailing industry expert and mobile detailer, in an article in *Modern Car Care* magazine. "Part of this stems from the cost of insurance and part of it from lack of understanding of the type of insurance you need. But without insurance, you are exposing yourself, your business, and your family to the gamble that nothing bad will ever happen while you are operating your business. But regardless of how careful you are or how good your intentions are, it only takes one accident or frivolous lawsuit to destroy your business, with all its earning potential."

St. Clair admits that in the early days of his detailing business, he operated without insurance. "But knowing what I know now, I would never be without insurance, regardless of the cost," he says.

Types of Insurance

Although there is insurance available to cover just about any situation imaginable, from negligence to property damage to glass breakage, no small-business owner can afford to insure against everything that can go wrong (Murphy's Law notwithstanding). Rather, you just have to assume some of the risk, then buy sufficient insurance to offset the more significant risk that would force your company into bankruptcy or cause serious financial problems. Generally speaking, the types of insurance detailers usually need are commercial garagekeeper's liability insurance, property insurance, and business interruption insurance. If you have employees, you also will need workers' compensation insurance.

Commercial Garagekeeper's Liability Insurance

This is the single most important type of coverage you will need for your detailing business. It covers damage to customers' vehicles, damage incurred if you're involved in an accident while driving a customer's vehicle, and injuries that happen at your place of business (including the injuries sustained by waiting customers who spill the cup of coffee they've been balancing dangerously on their knee). You may also need additional insurance, or a rider, if you send out mobile units from your fixed-site location.

Because you'll want your insurance to cover as much of the damage or lawsuit award as possible so your business will survive once a settlement has been made, it's imperative not to cheap out on the amount of coverage you buy. Insurance industry experts recommend obtaining $1 million to $2 million of garage liability coverage, which shouldn't break your piggy bank because it's not priced on a dollar-for-dollar basis. Rather, it's usually based on the size of your business (including factors like square footage of your facility, assets, and number of employees) and the risks involved in day-to-day operations. Also, as with car insurance, the higher your deductible, the more affordable the insurance becomes.

> **Tip...**
>
> ## Smart Tip
> Commercial garage-keeper's liability insurance for a detailer who owns property should run about $2,000 per bay per year, according to auto reconditioning industry consultant Prentice St. Clair. A detailer with no employees should expect to pay about $1,200 a year.

Property Insurance

Also known as casualty insurance, property insurance protects both the building you're working out of (if you own it) and its contents. Among the incidents property insurance can protect against are major disasters (like acts of God), fire, vandalism, and so on, and the amount of coverage possible is determined by the value of the property. The insurance company usually will send an appraiser out to place a value on the property before giving a quote.

Business Interruption Insurance

If the unthinkable happens and you're unable to operate due to a natural disaster or a fire, theft, or other insured loss, business interruption insurance will pay the cost of your normal business expenses. In addition to covering lost income, it may cover expenses like equipment replacement, facility rental, and so on. The price is determined by how likely you are to face certain risks. For instance, the premium cost could be higher for a detailer because you'll be storing flammable materials (like sprays and polishes). However, because it's possible for most detailers to work out of a temporary location while their facility is being repaired, interruption insurance costs may be somewhat lower than those of, say, a restaurant, which would be out of business if it was shuttered for some reason. Talk to your insurance broker about whether you should have this insurance and how much it would cost.

Workers' Compensation Insurance

You are entitled to make some decisions when it comes to the other types of insurance discussed so far, but you don't have that luxury with workers' compensation insurance. Forty-nine states require employers to have workers' comp, which covers employees who have work-related injuries, diseases, and illnesses. (In Texas, the employers themselves are permitted to decide whether or not to provide workers' comp.) It's considered to be "no-fault" insurance, meaning the employer doesn't have to admit responsibility for any injury or illness, and the employee doesn't have to sue to get compensation.

> **Fun Fact**
>
> The Uniform Work-men's Compensation Law, which was enacted to protect workers who are injured on the job, was created in 1910. In the ensuing 50 years, every state adopted some version of the law. Hawaii was the last state aboard.

Workers' comp insurance is such a complicated issue that it can't be handled in depth in this guide. But here are a few details you should know:

- Most states allow employers to purchase workers' comp through private insurance carriers. However, a few states require them to buy it through a state fund instead. For a list of those states, go to the U.S. Department of Labor's table at www.dol.gov/esa/regs/statutes/owcp/stwclaw/tables-pdf/table-1.pdf.

- The amount of coverage necessary and the percentage of salary paid to employees under workers' comp varies by state. In Michigan, for example, an employee receives 80 percent of his/her spendable earnings while on leave for a temporary disability. Your insurance broker can fill you in on the details relating to your situation.

- Premiums also vary by state and are influenced by factors like payroll size, your industry (the more hazardous the industry, the higher the rate), and the severity of potential work injuries.

- The owner doesn't count as an employee under workers' comp law, so you're not covered by workers' comp. Because you're on your own, you should seriously consider buying business interruption insurance and paying the premiums on a personal health insurance policy.

Other Types of Insurance

As mentioned previously, you can get insurance to guard against just about any kind of risk. Other types to consider include:

- *Bonding insurance.* This protects you against loss incurred by employees who steal, either from you or your customers.

- *Disability insurance.* If you can't work due to injury or illness, this insurance will replace a percentage of your gross income. Self-employed people do not qualify for workers' comp insurance (because they're considered the employer of record, even if they don't actually have employees), so this is the way to go to make sure you have money coming in while you're recuperating.

- *Health insurance.* Beginning with the 2003 income tax filing year, the IRS allows a health-insurance-premiums deduction of 100 percent for self-employed people who report a net profit on Schedule C, C-EZ, or F. The cost of medical and dental insurance, as well as qualified long-term care insurance for yourself, your spouse, and your dependents all qualify for the deduction. (Here's where you need that accountant to make sure you take the deduction properly.) See IRS Publication 535, *Business Expenses,* for more information. By the way, offering health insurance to employees can be a good recruiting and retention tool, and those premiums are also deductible.

- *Life insurance.* In addition to protecting your family or significant other in case of your death, you may need a life insurance policy if you're planning to seek financing. It's not uncommon for banks to require business owners to have life insurance before they'll show them the money.

As you can see, an insurance broker really is invaluable for wading through the morass of insurance policies and options, then helping you decide which ones are right for you. To help you along, we've included an insurance planning worksheet on page 58 that you can use to compare policies and premiums.

Tip...

Smart Tip

In the event of a loss, good insurance records are crucial. So be sure to keep receipts for every item purchased for the business; keep a written inventory of each item with the date of purchase, price, and current value; and either photograph or videotape the contents of each room. Then keep these documents in a safe place (like a safe deposit box), not in your shop.

▲

Business Insurance Planning Worksheet

Type	Required	Annual Cost
Commercial garagekeeper's liability		
Property		
Business interruption		
Workers' compensation	yes	
Bonding		
Disability		
Health		
Life		
Other		
Total Annual Cost		$

Detailing Tools
and Toys

Are you the type of person who gleefully wanders the aisles of an automotive superstore with eyes glazed over by the dizzying array of products to choose from? Do you pore over auto supply catalogs the same way kids memorize the toy section of the JC Penney Christmas catalog? Or do power tools—especially big, loud ones—send you into paroxysms of joy? Then you've definitely selected the right profession.

Detailers get to have all kinds of raucous fun with tools like gleaming stainless-steel power sprayers, rotary buffers that can polish a coconut to billiard-ball smoothness, and pressure washers that can repel an armadillo at ten paces. Then, add your choice of all the waxes, dressings, and polishes you could ever dream of to restore the showroom shine to even the oldest battle cruiser, and you have a profession to dye carpet for.

In this chapter, we've included typical prices for the higher priced items you may need to give you an idea of what you'll be spending, whether you're site-based or mobile. Equipment specific to mobile detailers is listed in its own section. To give you an idea of how typical expenses may add up, you'll find equipment and supplies cost breakdowns for two hypothetical companies on pages 72–73. Details on Wheels is a one-person sole proprietorship, while Executive Auto Restoration & Detail is a C corporation with one full-time employee (the owner), two part-time technicians, and a three-bay, 3,000-square-foot detailing shop in a large metropolitan area. You'll also find an equipment and supplies worksheet on pages 74–75 that you can use to start jotting down your own business expenses.

Now, here's a rundown of all the equipment and supplies you may need to indulge your inner gearhead.

Power Tools and Accessories

Among the must-haves for either a fixed-site or mobile detailer are:

- *Air compressor.* This is for powering pneumatic tools ($400).
- *Random orbital polisher.* Go for pneumatic if you're going to install a compressed-air system; otherwise, electric is fine. In addition to buffing, this can be used to shampoo carpet and floor mats simply by using a brush attachment. They run about $150. Bonnets are used on this piece of equipment to remove cleaners, polish, wax, and other sealants. There are many to choose from at various prices, most under $10.
- *Variable-speed rotary buffer/polisher.* Available in pneumatic and electric versions, this tool creates friction and heat so surface irregularities can be corrected and a high shine can be achieved. They run $200. The cutting and finishing pads you need for this tool are available at various prices, generally under $10.
- *Pressure washer.* Experts recommend buying the highest-quality pressure washer you can afford because it will last longer and do

> **Tip...**
>
> **Smart Tip**
>
> Because you'll use your rotary buffer every day, consider buying a pneumatic model. They're not as heavy as the electric versions, so you won't get as tired after using it for a few hours. A variable-speed model that goes from 600 to 2,400 rpm is a versatile choice.

a better job. Excellent for engine detailing, they start at about $900, but a really sweet model can be as much as $2,500.

- *Stainless-steel tank sprayer.* This is for dispensing everything except acid. A three-gallon sprayer is the perfect size for a mobile operation and runs around $139. A five-gallon model is around $150. A tank cart for easily wheeling this type of sprayer to the work site runs $125 to $175.

Beware!
Always buy the best tools you can afford and use them only in the way they're intended. The wrong cleaning tool can cause major damage, like surface scratches or paint damage that can take hours to repair.

- *Vapor steam cleaner.* This is for power cleaning and deodorizing. They run $400 to $1,200.

- *Carpet extractor.* This pulls shampoo and rinse water out of carpeting and is preferred by professionals over wet-dry vacs because it has better suction power and thus prevents mildew in carpeting. A professional extractor will run about $1,300.

- *Wet-dry vacuum.* This is the alternative to a carpet extractor. You'll need at least a five-hp motor or it won't have enough power. This runs about $355.

- *Ozone odor remover.* This device is for removing many odors, including tobacco smoke, spoiled food, mildew, pet deposits, and so on. It runs about $379.

- *Odor fogger system.* Used before shampooing to remove a wide variety of odors, the fogger disperses chemicals into a vehicle's interior to neutralize noxious odors, including smoke, food, mold and mildew, and pet accidents. The complete kit is about $350.

Additional tools that are particularly useful for detailers include a creeper for sliding under vehicles ($170); a temperature gauge for checking the temperature of paint ($80); a digital electronic or magnetic paint-thickness gauge, which helps you determine how much buffing the clearcoat can withstand ($500); and a photographer's loupe for getting a close-up view of flaws in the paint ($7). An interior dryer ($175) and a towel wringer ($120) are also great helpers for auto detailers.

Cleaning Products and Tools

Because prices can vary widely on cleaning products, we've provided you with a checklist, on page 63, of the numerous chemicals and other products you'll need. The Appendix has a list of suppliers you can check out when you're ready to buy.

It's also worth mentioning the initial costs of the various add-on services that can add hundreds of dollars to the cost of a basic detail yet have very low per-application materials costs. For instance, small vinyl and leather repairs cost less than $5, yet you can charge $25 to $75. Among these add-ons (and their costs to get started) are:

- Paintless dent repair (around $2,000 to $10,000 for a turnkey system with training)
- Paint touch-up (requires hands-on training to do well—$1,500 to $3,000)
- Vinyl and leather repair ($300 to $1,000)
- Carpet and fabric repair ($300 to $700)
- Carpet dyeing ($375)
- Gold-plating ($1,500 to $3,000)
- Windshield repair ($500 to $2,500)

Although this probably looks like a lot of stuff to buy, you'll find that the highest costs are for the power tools. Luckily, your equipment should last a long time if you buy high-quality tools. To really keep your costs down, check out online auction sites like eBay, where you can get some great bargains. For instance, a used Honda generator with low "mileage" that costs around $1,800 new was recently listed for $800. Everything else, from brushes to chemicals, is far less expensive, even if you do need a lot of items when you start out. But overall, you'll find your supply costs will be pretty low from month to month, particularly when you consider just how much you can earn from them.

Now let's move on to some other detailing necessities.

> **Bright Idea**
>
> Window tinting is another add-on service that can bring in big bucks for detailers. However, the skill is difficult to learn—curved windows are the hardest—and the job can take up to four hours to complete. A lot of detailers prefer to outsource this work and then mark up the service to make a few bucks.

Fast Track to Detail Success

Auto detailing and reconditioning systems help you get a fast start in the business by providing you with all the right equipment, support, and training as a package deal. Here are a few to consider if you're interested in this approach:

○ *Detail King.* This company offers auto detailing business start-up packages that include equipment, supplies, training, and marketing support (www. detailking.com).

○ *Detail Plus Car Appearance Systems.* In addition to offering one of the most complete detailing and express detailing systems around, Detail Plus also has supplies, chemicals, and equipment (www.detailplus.com).

○ *National Detail Systems.* This company is known for auto detailing systems; mobile auto repair and reconditioning systems; as well as detailing products and equipment, training, and support; and has an online superstore for detailing supplies and car-care equipment (www.nationaldetail.com).

Cleaning Products and Tools Checklist

Interior Cleaning Products
- ❑ Carpet shampoo, protectant
- ❑ Upholstery shampoo, protectant
- ❑ Spot remover
- ❑ Deodorizer and disinfectant
- ❑ Fogger bombs (a less expensive alternative to an ozone odor remover or odor fogger system)
- ❑ Cotton-tipped applicators (also used on the exterior to clean tight spots, like around taillight lenses)
- ❑ Vinyl cleaner, dressing, protectant, dyes
- ❑ Leather cleaner, conditioner, dyes
- ❑ Clear plastic cleaner

Exterior Cleaning Products
- ❑ Exterior shampoo
- ❑ Detailing clay
- ❑ Buffing compounds in various grits
- ❑ Tar/grease remover
- ❑ Wax and silicone remover
- ❑ Presoak bug remover
- ❑ Decal remover
- ❑ Paint leveler (an acid rain/scratch remover)
- ❑ Carnauba and synthetic wax
- ❑ Vinyl and convertible top cleaner
- ❑ Microfine sandpaper grit (for color sanding, removing surface scratches)
- ❑ Glass polish
- ❑ Aluminum polish
- ❑ Chrome polish
- ❑ Wheel cleaner, dressing, polish
- ❑ Rubber and black trim restorer
- ❑ Masking tape (to cover door, hood, trunk edges where paint is thin to prevent burning through it)

- ❑ Tire cleaner, dressing, protectant
- ❑ Engine degreaser
- ❑ WD-40

Cleaning Tools
- ❑ Wheel/tire brush
- ❑ Spoke and slot brush
- ❑ Vent brush
- ❑ Carpet/fabric brush
- ❑ Sponge (natural)
- ❑ Spray and squeeze bottles
- ❑ Nylon bug/tar sponge
- ❑ Cotton- or foam-tipped applicators (for crevice cleaning)
- ❑ Engine detail brush
- ❑ Single-edge razor blades
- ❑ Chamois (natural chamois absorbs more water)
- ❑ Dry cleaning cloths (for removing film, dirt)
- ❑ Terrycloth towels (Detailing experts recommend having a different color for each application, including application and buffing of products, products with silicone, window washing, interior cleaning, etc.)
- ❑ Microfiber towels (now a favorite among detailers because they're softer and lint-free)
- ❑ Feather duster
- ❑ Squeegee
- ❑ Paper floor mats, seat covers

Miscellaneous
- ❑ Creeper (for sliding easily under a vehicle)
- ❑ Towel wringer
- ❑ Interior dryer

Personal Protection Equipment

Anyone who works with power equipment for an extended period every day should consider wearing ear protection. Although an internet search didn't turn up any decibel-level information for specific detailing tools, it is known that shop tools operate at up to 90 decibels, according to Quiet Solution, a manufacturer of soundproofing products, whereas pneumatic drills operate at 110 decibels. OSHA says that since hearing damage can occur with even limited exposure to sound levels in the 85 to 90 dB range, hearing protection is recommended. You can pick up headset-style hearing protectors for around $15 a pair.

Safety glasses are a good idea for protecting sensitive eyes from airborne chemicals and particles. They're a bargain at about $5 a pair.

Uniforms and Hats

To increase the professionalism of your business, detailers should always wear clean, wrinkle-free uniform shirts while on the job. While a uniform company like Cintas can provide you with fresh uniforms, that can be expensive, especially for a one- or two-person detailing business. Instead, you can adopt embroidered polo shirts with collars as your company uniform. (Avoid T-shirts; they look too casual.) Personalized shirts (and baseball caps for mobile detailers) not only give you a neat, professional appearance, but they are also a low-cost advertising tool. And here's an added bonus: The IRS considers shirts that have your company name and logo on them to be advertising and will allow you to deduct their cost. Embroidered polo shirts cost as little as $15 each, and hats run $12 to $17 each. You don't have to buy a lot of them to get this kind of pricing, either; some companies will sell you as few as six shirts at a time.

"Uniforms are a must," says Dave Echnoz of 14/69 Carwash Supercenter in Fort Wayne, Indiana. "The stereotypical detailer is a guy with a bandana, cut-offs and a Budweiser in his hand who cusses all the time. Customers don't trust that kind of guy—they're going to worry if their Palm Pilot is still in the glove compartment after the work is done. So you have to look good on the job."

Echnoz also recommends paying just half of the uniform cost for full-time employees so they won't expect new shirts all the time. "And unless Nike is going to cut you a check to wear their hat, don't wear Nike. Get a personalized company hat," he adds.

> **Tip...**
>
> **Smart Tip**
>
> Sunblock or a strong sunscreen is a must for mobile detailers. Studies show that prolonged exposure to the sun (particularly during the hours of 10 A.M. to 3 P.M.) increases your risk of developing skin cancer. So everyone should wear a minimum 15 SPF sunscreen while working outdoors.

Special Mobile Equipment

Although a mobile detailer will use many of the same tools and supplies listed earlier, there are a few other things you'll need to get into business. The very first thing is a reliable vehicle in good repair—preferably a pickup truck with a covered bed—for hauling around your equipment. Vehicles that double as family transportation, including vans and SUVs, also will work, but of course you'll have to remove your detailing equipment before the family can pile in for a trip to the mall. Many mobile detailers prefer to have a vehicle dedicated to the business, and because payment and maintenance costs are fully deductible business expenses, it's usually not too hard—even for the detailer operating on a shoestring—to swing this expense. A reliable used truck or van should cost around $5,000 to $6,000, plus you'll need about $5,000 to equip it. If you prefer to go new, you can buy a low-end truck for around $14,000.

Among the items you'll have to carry in your truck are a portable 125-gallon water tank (enough for a full day of washing), which will run about $279; a pressure washer ($900 to $2,500); a wet-dry vacuum ($355) or carpet extractor ($1,300); a variable-speed buffer ($200); and a generator to operate all your equipment (about $1,800). A better way to tote around all that equipment is with a detailing trailer that attaches to the back of your vehicle. For $5,500 to $8,000, you can get a trailer complete with a water tank, pressure washer, generator, air compressor, and toolbox—almost everything you'll need except supplies. You'll also need to carry a sufficient supply of detailing supplies, like brushes, and enough towels and chemicals to carry you through the day. Other useful items include portable florescent lighting for peering into those hard-to-see nooks and crannies under the hood ($195), and a portable space heater ($130) for when the temperature dips or you're forced to work after the sun goes down.

A portable pop-up tent is also a good idea for protecting yourself and your customers' cars from the elements, including sudden rain and excessive heat (which can affect the way certain products adhere to the paint). These tents are discussed in greater detail in Chapter 7, but for now, you can pencil $1,000 into your start-up cost worksheet if you think a tent is a good idea.

If you really have to use the family van/SUV/truck for your business, you may want to invest in a mobile rig that can be hooked to the back of your vehicle during business hours. These rigs can carry everything you need and may include a water tank, a pressure washer, pressurized hoses, chemical dispensers and other tools. They run anywhere from $3,000 to

Smart Tip

Tip...

Although mobile detailing is a huge convenience for customers, it wastes time for the detailer because drive time is not billable. So whenever possible, schedule jobs in the same area for the same day, or arrange to be in a central location, like an office complex, for an entire day.

$5,000. Add on a mobile wash system for $2,200, and you're ready to detail anything that gets in your way. Other companies sell systems that can be skid-mounted in the back of a truck.

Finally, mobile detailers need a wastewater reclamation system to capture water runoff so chemicals don't wind up in municipal storm sewers. Although this is an EPA requirement, many mobile detailers ignore the law and go on their merry way, polluting the water. But don't do it. In addition to harming Mother Earth, you could be subject to stiff fines if the municipality where you do business finds out you're not reclaiming the water properly. Not to mention it doesn't look very professional working in the center of an office complex parking lot with a lake of water all around the car you're detailing.

Wastewater reclamation systems consist of a flexible tube with a flat bottom that is adhered to surfaces like concrete using a vacuum. This forms an impenetrable barrier where wastewater can collect. This water is then vacuumed up and discharged into a holding tank so it can later be poured into any sanitary sewer—even your toilet. These systems start at around $2,400 for a system that can be used when runoff is in one direction, or $3,400 for a closed-loop system that completely surrounds the vehicle.

Other things you'll need to run a mobile business include office furniture for your home workspace; office equipment and supplies, including a computer, printer, phone, and answering machine; business cards; and uniforms. Each of these items is discussed in the site-based requirements information that follows.

Fixed-Location Bays, Fixtures, and Furniture

In addition to all the equipment you'll need, you have to outfit the facility to make the work areas functional and the customer areas comfortable. For the purpose of this discussion, we'll assume you'll be working in a building that has automotive bays. So the only other requirements are good overhead lighting, plenty of electrical outlets, convenient water sources, and enough drains of the correct size in the floor to meet code, all of which should be in the facility already

---

Tip...

Smart Tip

Because mobile equipment takes more of a beating than site-based tools, it requires constant care and maintenance to keep it in top condition. Also, remember to detail your own tools and vehicle regularly so your image is as neat and professional as the work you do.

Tip...

Smart Tip

For a more professional detailing environment, consider installing in-shop detailing workstations like the Chemspense system sold by Detail Plus Car Appearance Systems (www.detailplus.com). It neatly holds a wet-dry vacuum; heated soil extractor; coiled lines for operating pneumatic buffers, shampooers, and orbital waxers; and chemical lines for product dispensing.

if it was previously used to provide automotive services. You'll also need a properly functioning sewer system with a sand trap and oil separator, which is required by local ordinances and the EPA. For a further discussion of these requirements, see Chapter 7.

Finally, it would be much appreciated by your employees if you designate a small area in the service room for breaks. A couple of chairs and maybe a small table where employees can put down their soft drinks or coffee are all that's necessary for someone taking a break from buffing and polishing duties. Alternatively, you could put a couple of guest chairs in your office for the same purpose, as long as there's enough room and you don't mind sharing the space with chattering breakers.

Waiting Room Necessities

Even though your work area will be the heart of your operation if you have a fixed location, your waiting room is a very important part of your detail shop. To make it comfortable for anyone who must wait for his/her vehicle, put in three to four matching chairs (the padded vinyl chairs sold as "visitors' chairs" at office supply or restaurant supply stores are a good choice and are quite reasonably priced at about $100 each). Other welcome amenities include a coffeemaker and a table to hold it (about $100 for both at an office supply store), a wall-mounted TV ($150 for a new 19" color TV and $100 for the mounting bracket), and a magazine rack ($100) filled with a variety of reading materials. A display area for retail products (a simple bookcase or wall-mounted shelves will do) and holders for your service brochure and your business cards are also necessary for the waiting room. (Brochure holders run about $10 each and business card holders are around $5.) You'll also need a stool for behind the service counter ($90). And just in case you're wondering, it's not necessary to have a cash register in most detail shops. People who are spending $150 or more for detailing are more likely to use a credit card or write a check than dole out the cash. You might want to invest in a locking cash box for your desk drawer, where you can stash checks, credit card slips, and the occasional Jacksons and Grants until you cash out at the end of the business day.

Finally, you should seriously consider investing in a washer and dryer for on-site laundering of towels, detailing aprons, and other items. The last thing you want to do is take those chemical-laden and dirt-encrusted towels home and wash them in the same machine you use for your Jockeys. A low-end Kenmore washer/dryer pair from Sears will cost only about $500 new, but of course you might also be able to find reliable appliances through the classified ads or a used appliance dealer.

Office Equipment and Furniture

Both site and mobile detailers have simple needs when it comes to outfitting an office. In the case of a facility-based detailer, your office will house your computer and a printer for creating receipts, as well as credit card processing equipment. The sole exception to this rule would probably be if your office is located so far away from the waiting room that it would be inconvenient for your customers to wait for you to make the trip there and back. If the office is too far away, you could place the credit card equipment out of sight behind the counter.

Speaking of processing credit card transactions, you have a number of options for handling the task. The most common way is with a point-of-sale (POS) terminal (starting at around $299), coupled with a credit card receipt printer ($195). If space is at a premium, you can opt instead for a terminal like the Hypercom T7P Standard, which has a thermal printer built right in so you don't need a separate receipt printer. This type of POS unit starts at around $329. There are even wireless POS terminals, like the Nurit 3010, that are perfect for mobile detailers. They start at around $995, and you'll need cellular phone service to power them.

Finally, if you don't want to invest in any additional equipment at all, you can purchase PC- or MAC-based POS software that works with your desktop computer. A few packages to check out include PcCharge Pro (GO Software Inc., $395), POSitive Basic (POSitive Software, $299), Chargem Software (Capital Merchant Solutions, $349), and ICVerify (ICVerify, $199). You'll find the names of companies that sell both POS equipment and software in the Appendix under "Point-of-Sale Equipment" and "Point-of-Sale Software."

And by the way, all this equipment and software is great, but only if you've established a merchant account that will allow you to use it. A merchant account is an electronic clearinghouse for your credit and debit transactions. Typically it costs $100 to establish a new merchant account, and then you'll pay a variety of fees every month to process transactions through the POS equipment discussed above. See Chapter 13 for a more detailed discussion of merchant accounts.

Your basic office furniture needs will include a desk or computer workstation, a comfortable office chair (preferably one that's ergonomic to minimize back discomfort), and a sturdy two- or four-drawer file cabinet. Since your customers will never see your office, feel free to furnish it with inexpensive or secondhand furniture, just as long as it's in good condition. If you go new, check out office supply stores like Staples or Office Depot, which sell reasonably priced desks for just $200 to $600, and chairs for $60 to $250. Ready-to-assemble furniture is also quite affordable, as is used furniture, which you can find through newspaper classified ads. A two-drawer, letter-size file cabinet costs as little as $25, although the $100 model may be the better buy because its drawers extend fully, making it easier to remove file folders from the very back. See the Office Equipment Worksheet on page 77.

Mobile detailers also need a specific place to handle paperwork and make phone calls, but of course that space will be in your home rather than in a shop. That space should be dedicated just to your business, not shared with an Xbox or the laundry. Make sure you let your children know this is your "special place" and that your computer, desk, fax machine, etc., are not for their entertainment.

Personal Computer

There's no question that a desktop computer is a necessity for this business. In addition to churning out receipts, you can use a computer to write checks to suppliers, balance your budget, create promotional materials, and so on. Computer systems are often advertised for as little as $699, although by the time you add on a monitor, mouse, modem, printer and supplies, a complete Pentium-based system will run around $2,000 to $4,000.

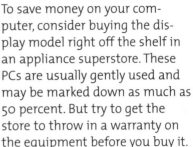

Dollar Stretcher

To save money on your computer, consider buying the display model right off the shelf in an appliance superstore. These PCs are usually gently used and may be marked down as much as 50 percent. But try to get the store to throw in a warranty on the equipment before you buy it.

To run the most common business software packages, your system should have a speed of 2.2GHz, with at least 40GB memory and 256MB SDRAM. It should come equipped with a CD-RW drive, so you can load most software packages and download data to CD, as well as internal fax and modem cards. Other optional equipment that's nice to have includes a scanner for scanning in photos of cars you've detailed (which ranges from $150 to $300, depending on the resolution) and a Zip drive ($100 to $200) for long-term data records storage.

Software

While there are many general office productivity and business software packages on the market, Microsoft Office and Intuit QuickBooks are the standards. Microsoft Office Professional includes word processing, spreadsheet, database management, e-mail, and presentation programs and retails for $499. Intuit's QuickBooks is an easy-to-use accounting package that not only keeps your financial records but also can manage your business checking account and print checks. QuickBooks Basic retails for $199.95.

To date, there isn't a software package made specifically for auto detailers. The closest things are the packages created for carwashes and auto dealerships that have detailing departments. But there's no need to go to the expense of buying one of those programs when Office and QuickBooks will do everything you need.

Fax Machine

Now that computers come equipped with fax cards, full-size fax machines are becoming less common. That's also why the prices have dropped so much, to as little as $150 for a multifunction machine that also scans, copies, and prints. If you decide to install your fax machine on a dedicated telephone line, the installation fee will run $40 to $60, plus you'll incur the cost of the monthly phone service. If you use your computer fax card, you'll still need a separate phone line to run it on, plus you'll have to leave your computer on 24/7 so it's always ready to receive incoming messages.

Telephones, Answering Machines, and Pagers

Make sure you buy the best model you can afford since you and your staff will be using the phone constantly. A standard two-line speakerphone with autoredial, memory dial, flashing lights, mute button, and other useful features will run $70 to $150, while a top-of-the-line model can cost $250 or more. A great source for high-quality phones is Hello Direct (see the Appendix), which carries the Polycom line of professional business telephones.

A stand-alone answering machine costs $40 to $150, while a cordless phone/answering machine combo runs $50 to nearly $200. Buy the best you can afford so it will serve you well.

Although a cellular phone isn't really a necessity for a detailer, practically everyone has one these days, so chances are you do, too. If your cell is used strictly for business, it's 100 percent deductible on your business taxes. New cellular service starts at about $20 a month for a minimum number of minutes, to as much as $70 for the Cadillac of phone packages. The cell phone itself will run up to $200 for the coolest models or under $100 for a Plain Jane model. Some cellular companies (like T-Mobile) still offer a free phone with service activation.

Finally, pagers are a handy way to keep in touch with your employees, and they're very inexpensive these days. A lot of paging service providers will throw in a basic pager when you activate the service. Otherwise, a new pager costs as little as $30 from sources like Beepers.com (see the Appendix). As with cellular service, there are tons of service plans to choose from.

Copy Machines

Having a copy machine in your office is a real convenience, although not a necessity for most detailers. If you think you need one, pick up a compact personal copier from an office superstore for as little as $150, which gives you just basic copy functions. If you have big jobs, like printing 1,000 fliers, take them someplace like Kinko's for reproducing. Supplies you'll need for your copier include copy paper and toner cartridges. Both are readily available from your local office supply store; the cartridges sell for around $90.

Office Supplies

You're going to need a supply of pens, paper, Post-Its®, file folders, and other office supplies to do business. About $30 a month should cover anything you'll need.

Another necessary start-up cost is for business cards, brochures, and service menus (a brochure-sized document that has the prices of all the services you offer). A quick-print shop like American Speedy Printing or an online printing company like Color-PrintingCentral.com can design and produce all these items for you. (We've listed a few companies under "Printing Resources" in the Appendix.) To get the most competitive quote, you can use an online source like Print Quote USA. All you do is type in the specs for your job, and the web site will do the rest. A casual price survey revealed that 1,000 full-color 8.5-by-11-inch brochures printed on good quality paper can run around $350.

The major office supply stores are a good source for professional-looking yet inexpensive business cards. They start at around $25 for 1,000 one-color business cards on laid stock, which is sturdy and conservative.

Security Equipment

If you plan to allow customers to drop off vehicles before the shop opens or the night before they're serviced, you'll need to invest in a reliable security system. Probably the best choice for a detailing shop is a silent alarm, which is connected to a monitoring station that notifies the police when the alarm is tripped. Perimeter or entry alarms sound if someone tries to enter your shop, whereas space protection alarms use infrared beams or motion detectors to detect whether someone is in your facility illegally. The least effective type is local alarms, which aren't connected to an alarm company monitoring station or police department but are loud and can attract unwanted attention—if anyone really cares enough to report the blaring alarm. Whichever system you choose, pick one with a battery or other backup in case of a power failure.

Often a combination of alarm types is necessary to protect your property adequately. A combination package may cost $500 to $2,000, and an installed alarm can run $1,500 to $3,000. Consult the "Security Control Equipment and Systems" category in the Yellow Pages for security system vendors and installers.

The Moment of Truth

By now you should have a lot of entries on the Start-Up Expenses Worksheet on page 79. Try running the numbers now, and you'll have a pretty clear idea of how much capital it will take to get your business up and running. If you gulp when you see the total, check out Chapter 13 for advice on how to obtain start-up financing. For some hypothetical start-up expenses, take a look at page 78. This will give you an idea of what low-end to high-end start-up expenses might be.

Detailing Equipment and Supplies

Detailing Equipment and Supplies	Details on Wheels	Executive Auto Restoration & Detail
Detailing trailer*	$5,500	
Air compressor	$400	$400
Random orbital polisher		$300 **
Variable-speed rotary buffer/polisher	$200	$400 **
Pressure washer***		$2,500
125-gallon water tank***	$279	
5-gallon stainless-steel tank sprayer		$300 **
Ozone odor remover		$375
Odor fogger system	$350	
Carpet extractor		$1,300
Wet-dry vacuum	$355	
Vapor steam cleaner		$1,200
Interior dryer	$175	$175
Creeper	$170	$170
Temperature gauge	$80	$80
Digital electronic paint-thickness gauge		$500
Magnifier loupe	$7	$14
Towels	$50	$100
Towel wringer		$120
Generator***		$1,800
Portable florescent lighting		$195
Portable space heater	$130	
Portable pop-up tent	$1,000	
Wastewater reclamation system	$2,400	
Miscellaneous detailing tools	$300	$500
Miscellaneous detailing products	$300	$800
Magnetic signage	$60	$60
Washer, dryer		$500

Detailing Equipment and Supplies, continued

Waiting room furniture/equipment		
Service counter stool		$90
Visitor chairs (4)		$400
Retail product display		$100
Magazine rack		$100
TV set		$150
TV mounting bracket		$100
Coffeemaker/table		$100
Point-of-sale terminal	$995	$329
Brochure/business card holders		$15
Retail products and supplies		
Initial inventory		$200
Total	$7,251	$13,373

*Basic rig with tailer, water tank, pressure washer, and generator
**Where noted, this price represents a quantity of two
***Not needed by mobile detailer if you go with a basic detailing rig

▲

Detailing Equipment and Supplies Worksheet

Detailing Equipment and Supplies	
Detailing trailer*	
Air compressor	
Random orbital polisher	
Variable-speed rotary buffer/polisher	
Pressure washer	
125-gallon water tank	
5-gallon stainless-steel tank sprayer	
Ozone odor remover	
Odor fogger system	
Carpet extractor	
Wet-dry vacuum	
Vapor steam cleaner	
Interior dryer	
Creeper	
Temperature gauge	
Digital electronic paint-thickness gauge	
Magnifier loupe	
Towels	
Towel wringer	
Generator**	
Portable florescent lighting	
Portable space heater	
Portable pop-up tent	
Wastewater reclamation system	
Miscellaneous detailing tools	
Miscellaneous detailing products	
Magnetic signage	
Washer, dryer	

Detailing Equipment and Supplies Worksheet, continued

Waiting room furniture/equipment	
Service counter stool	
Visitor chairs (4)	
Retail product display	
Magazine rack	
TV set	
TV mounting bracket	
Coffeemaker/table	
Point-of-sale terminal	
Brochure/business card holders	
Retail products and supplies	
Initial inventory	
Total	$

*Basic rig with trailer, water tank, pressure washer, and generator
**Not needed by mobile detailer if you go with a basic detailing rig*

Office Equipment and Supplies

Office Equipment	Details on Wheels	Executive Auto Restoration & Detail
Computer, printer	$2,000	$2,000
Surge protector	$20	$20
Multipurpose fax/scanner/copier		$150
Copy machine		$150
Phone	$70	$250
Cell phone	$100	$200
Pager		$30
Answering machine	$40	$70
Calculator	$25	$25
Security system		$2,000
Software		
Microsoft Office	$500	$500
Intuit QuickBooks	$200	$200
Office furniture		
Desk	$200	$300
Chair	$100	$250
File cabinet(s)	$100	$200
Bookcase(s)		$100
Office supplies		
Business cards	$25	$25
Service brochures	$350	$350
Miscellaneous supplies (pens, folders, etc.)	$30	$50
Computer/copier paper	$25	$25
Extra printer cartridges	$50	$50
Extra fax cartridges		$55
Extra copier toner		$90
CD-RW disks		$20
3.5-inch floppy disks	$7	
Mouse pad	$10	$10
Total	*$3,852*	*$7,120*

Office Equipment and Supplies Worksheet

Office Equipment	
Computer, printer	
Surge protector	
Multipurpose fax/scanner/copier	
Copy machine	
Phone	
Cell phone	
Pager	
Answering machine	
Calculator	
Security system	
Software	
Microsoft Office	
Intuit QuickBooks	
Office furniture	
Desk	
Chair	
File cabinet(s)	
Bookcase(s)	
Office supplies	
Business cards	
Service brochures	
Miscellaneous supplies (pens, folders, etc.)	
Computer/copier paper	
Extra printer cartridges	
Extra fax cartridges	
Extra copier toner	
CD-RW disks	
3.5-inch floppy disks	
Mouse pad	
Total	$

Start-Up Expenses

Item	Details on Wheels	Executive Auto Restoration & Detail
Mortgage (first six months)		$7,200
Detailing equipment, tools, supplies	$11,297	$13,518
Office equipment, furniture, supplies	$3,852	$7,120
Merchant account setup fee	$100	$100
Business licenses	$20	$20
Vehicle transport tag		$125
Phone (line installation charges)	$90	$115
Utility deposits		$150
Employee wages and benefits (first six months)		$11,440
Owner/employee uniform shirts, hats	$162	$180
Safety equipment (hearing, eye protection)	$20	$60
Start-up advertising	$100	$200
Legal services	$200	$900
Insurance (annual cost)	$1,500	$2,500
Market research	$250	$1,000
Membership dues	$225	$225
Publications (annual subscriptions)	$60	$300
Online service	$20	$20
Web site design	$800	$1,500
Web hosting, domain name	$90	$90
Subtotal	$18,786	$46,763
Miscellaneous expenses (roughly 10 percent of total)	$1,870	$4,670
Total	$20,656	$51,433

Start-Up Expenses Worksheet

Item	
Mortgage (first six months)	
Detailing equipment, tools, supplies	
Office equipment, furniture, supplies	
Merchant account set-up fee	
Business licenses	
Vehicle transport tag	
Phone (line installation charges)	
Utility deposits	
Employee wages and benefits (first six months)	
Owner/employee uniform shirts, hats	
Safety equipment (hearing, eye protection)	
Start-up advertising	
Legal services	
Insurance (annual cost)	
Market research	
Membership dues	
Publications (annual subscriptions)	
Online service	
Web site design	
Web hosting, domain name	
Subtotal	
Miscellaneous expenses (roughly 10 percent of total)	
Total	$

7

A Garage for All Seasons
Housing Your Business

Up to this point, we've discussed business basics that could apply to both mobile detailers and site-based detailers. Now let's zero in on the main difference between the two types of detailers: the actual space where you'll do business, whether it's truly space or a brick-and-mortar facility, as well as the places you can store your equipment and supplies.

Mobile Machinations

As we mentioned earlier, if you're interested in a start-up with the lowest possible costs, then mobile is the way to go because no facility is necessary. A mobile detailer's major fixed costs generally consist only of detailing equipment and some form of transportation (van, truck, SUV, or trailer) to get the equipment where the business is. But you'll still need a place to park all that equipment and your vehicle when they're not in use. And by the way, that shady spot on the street in front of your house is *not* an option—many cities and townships have ordinances that prohibit parking commercial vehicles and/or equipment rigs in the street.

The garage at your home is the logical place to store everything if you can spare the space. All you'll need is some steel shelving from a home improvement store like Home Depot so you can organize polishes, towels, and other supplies and keep them close at hand. To get your rig off the street when it's not in use, consider renting a unit in a self-storage facility. A space as small as 150 square feet, which is about the size of a large bedroom, should be sufficient for all your equipment and supplies. If you want to park your entire trailer inside, however, you'll need about 200 square feet (the size of a small one-car garage). Self-storage rental runs about $100 to $200 a month.

Because unexpected rainfall, surprise snow flurries, and extremely hot weather can adversely affect the way polishes and finishes seal on the vehicles you detail, you might consider investing in a portable pop-up tent that you can set up easily at the first sign of any weather that threatens your hard work. These canopies are so lightweight and easy to transport that some manufacturers recommend adding tent sandbags to make sure the tent itself doesn't take flight. A 10-by-20-foot tent that covers a 200-square-foot area runs around $1,000, and a set of six ready-to-use sandbags is about $80. The minimal shelter provided by this type of canopy also is effective for protecting yourself against UVA and UVB rays, which is always advisable because too much sun exposure can increase your risk of developing skin cancer.

A canopy also can come in handy for setting up a temporary detailing location, such as in a parking lot or office complex, where you can service drive-up customers. (Just be sure to obtain permission from the parking or building management company before unfurling your canopy.) Other places where a temporary location might work are swap meets and classic car shows—basically, any place where car aficionados

Beware!
More care and maintenance is needed for the tools and equipment used by a mobile operator than those used in a facility-based detailing business. Specialty equipment like compressors, power generators, and water reclamation equipment all need regular maintenance to make sure they don't go down when you have a book full of appointments.

congregate. If you have the option of having the canopy emblazoned with your company name, take it. It's great advertising at a reasonable cost.

To set up a temporary location, you'll need the same equipment as a mobile detailer, including water tanks, a power generator, and other accoutrements. Also, like a mobile detailer, you may have to relocate occasionally to get enough business. On the other hand, you won't spend as much time every day driving from job site to job site as you do when you're truly mobile.

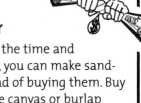
Shop Talk

A lot of detailers—including those who work in northern climates, where the weather can be fickle or downright lousy three-quarters of the year—choose to work out of a specialized detailing shop. The disadvantage is there are many more start-up costs when you have a fixed location, plus someone has to be at the shop all the time in case a customer stops by for unscheduled work, to make an appointment, or to buy do-it-yourself detailing products. The advantage is you could make a lot more money than you could as a mobile detailer, assuming you pick a good location and hire the right employees. Even in northern climes, where detailing business drops off in the winter, you can still find work among those auto aficionados who keep their rides showroom-perfect no matter what the weather (or perhaps *because* of the weather) as well as from dealers who use detailers to prep new vehicles and restore used and off-lease vehicles. As mentioned previously, there's even a thriving market for boat and airplane detailing, and winter might be a good time to promote that part of your business.

Location, Location, Location

Your detailing shop should be located in a commercial area that's easily accessible by highway or byway, preferably one that has plenty of traffic because that gives you added visibility. The building should have sufficient adjacent parking if at all possible, and the surrounding area should be well-maintained, well-lighted and safe.

Another desirable location is an auto mall, both because the new- and used-car dealers that anchor such malls are often frequent consumers of detailing work themselves and because there will be a steady stream of car shoppers in the area who could be prospective detailing customers. Likewise, a location in a mini-mall that has noncompeting automotive businesses, like tire stores, brake shops, vehicle alarm installers, and so on, can bring you great visibility and increased sales. Finally, a free-standing building located on the perimeter or "outlot" of a shopping center or mall, like those used by the national quick-lube franchises, could be an ideal choice.

Building Basics

Your first decision concerning your detailing facility should be whether you're up to the challenge of renovating an existing building or whether you'd prefer to move into a garage or gas station that's either defunct or for sale. (We won't even consider building a new facility as an option—it's simply too expensive for most new detailing entrepreneurs.) Renovation can be very expensive, so generally speaking it's better to look for a building that previously served as an automotive service provider, such as a garage. The good news is that a lot of the infrastructure you'll need, including automobile bays, special electrical connections, and maybe even fixtures like a service counter may come with the building. The bad news is that there could be a really good reason why the previous owner moved out, like there's too much competition in the area, the location is crummy, or the previous owner had a poor reputation in the community. The same goes for a detailing or other automotive-type business that's currently in business but is up for sale.

If you're seriously interested in taking over an existing or now-defunct detailing shop, garage, or gas station, find out exactly why it's on the block. If the business for sale is a detailing shop that's still operating, observe its activities for a few days, noting daily volume and clientele. Also, determine the worth of any equipment or fixtures that will be left behind and decide whether you'll be able to use it. Finally, consider remodeling costs vs. the cost of starting with a blank slate in a different facility.

A word of warning about shuttered gas stations: During the Reagan administration, legislation was signed into law requiring owners of gas stations and other facilities that have underground storage tanks to monitor them for leakage and properly clean up contaminated sites. Tanks that were found to be leaking had to be permanently closed and the soil decontaminated, and, not surprisingly, the cost of doing this drove some service stations out of business. So before you purchase an abandoned gas station, ask about the condition of the underground storage tanks and the owner's compliance with EPA requirements, including monitoring and soil testing. The EPA estimates that 225,000 sites in the United States are contaminated by petroleum leakage, and you don't want to get stuck with a hefty bill for cleanup. For more information about the initiative to clean up underground storage tanks (known as the Brownfields law), check out the EPA's web site at www.epa.gov/swerust1, or call the EPA hotline at (800) 424-9346.

Another potential problem with existing sites is that they may lack a properly functioning sewer system with a sand trap and oil separator, all of which are required by the EPA and many government agencies. All businesses are prohibited from discharging contaminants into the sewer system, so the sand trap and oil separator are required to remove sludge from water and divert it into a collection tank before the water is discharged into the sewer. The trouble is that it's not uncommon for buildings that have been used for automotive services to lack this very expensive system.

"It can cost a small fortune to retrofit a shop that doesn't have a working system, so I wouldn't even look at a shop that wasn't set up right," says Tom Schurmann, a 32-year detailing veteran in Lakewood, Colorado. "Some detailers ignore the rules, then find themselves in a major mess with city officials, the EPA and a multitude of government agencies."

To find an existing location for sale or lease (with or without the proper environmental protection equipment), check the advertising section of your local newspaper, or contact a real estate broker or rental agent.

At the Very Lease

Leasing can be a good way to go if you don't want the hassles of qualifying for a mortgage. But remember that a lease is a virtually unbreakable contract, no matter what happens to your business. For instance, if you sign a 36-month lease at $1,000 per month, you're liable for the full lease amount—$36,000—even if you move on to greener pastures (like a new facility or another line of work) before the lease is up. To protect yourself, try to negotiate a lease with the shortest term possible, like a one- or two-year lease with an option to renew for five years, so you have a way out if you need or want it. The option to renew is important—it prevents you from losing your lease and having to move suddenly. Just be aware that not every leasing company or landlord will agree to such short terms. You may have to keep looking for someone who will.

The types of leases you may encounter include flat leases, in which the price is set for a specific period of time, regardless of the landlord's expenses; step leases, in which the cost of your lease may go up annually as your landlord's taxes, insurance, and other costs increase; cost-of-living leases, which are adjusted annually based on the government's cost-of-living figures; and percentage leases, which consist of either a base rent amount or a percentage of the business's gross earnings, whichever is higher. The standard amount is 3 to 12 percent, usually paid on a quarterly basis, and you'll have to provide proof of your earnings. Turn around, and run if you encounter this kind of lease. Most new business owners can't afford a percentage lease in the early days of a new business.

▲

Buying versus Leasing

When you start looking at buildings, you'll find that the terms may vary widely, from assumable mortgages to short-term leases. In many cases, buying a building outright brings more benefits, including giving you more latitude when it comes to renovations and allowing you to control fixed costs like overhead, utilities, and (within reason) the terms of the mortgage. You'll also have the tax advantages of owning the building.

> **Tip...**
>
> **Smart Tip**
>
> When negotiating a lease for a lot of money, don't go it alone. Hire an attorney to look over the terms so you don't get burned. Among the things you'll want to negotiate are which additions or renovations are needed before the property is acceptable and the timetable for getting them done.

Leasing a free-standing building gives you some of the same advantages as buying, although you will have a landlord to deal with. But you can usually negotiate favorable terms upfront, so leasing is certainly a viable option.

Layout

A detailing facility has to be highly functional and have plenty of room to spread out in. Toward that end, you'll want to find a building around 2,000 square feet, which is enough space for two to three bays. If the building was previously used for a garage or other automotive-based business and has hoists, so much the better. But a building with standard service bays will work just fine. About 75 percent of the floor space should be allocated to the work area, which you'll want to line with shelving to store products and equipment. The rest of the building should be allocated for a manager's office (large enough for a small desk and a chair), a customer service area where clients can sit down until their vehicle is completed, a unisex restroom, and a storage area. You'll also have to find a place to stash the washer and dryer you'll need (you'll be doing a lot of towels, buffer pads, and other laundry). The trick is to find a place where the agitating and spinning won't be too noisy.

If you find the right size garage in a great location, but it doesn't have all these basic necessities, you should strongly consider doing some remodeling to include them. You'll find a sample layout for a 2,000-square-foot facility on page 87.

You'll want to keep all areas of the shop scrupulously clean. Seeing a cluttered detailing area or a messy manager's office could make customers question just how meticulous you'll be when detailing their prized rides.

> **Tip...**
>
> **Smart Tip**
>
> A bare concrete floor is acceptable for your waiting area if it's unstained and clean, but a durable floor covering like indoor-outdoor carpeting or tile is a good alternative. Be sure to select flooring in a neutral tone that will conceal dirt and blend with the wall color.

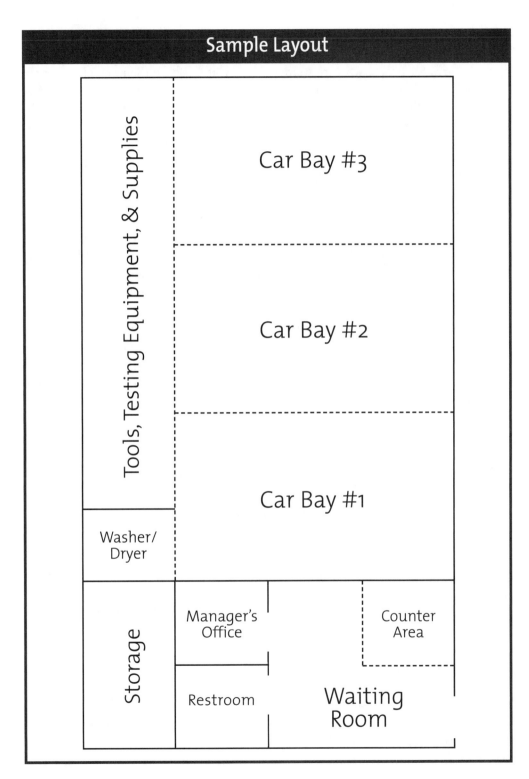

Sample Layout

Tools, Testing Equipment, & Supplies

Car Bay #3

Car Bay #2

Car Bay #1

Washer/ Dryer

Storage

Manager's Office

Restroom

Counter Area

Waiting Room

Likewise, the customer area should be neat and brightly lit, and the furniture must be comfortable and in good repair. Put a few auto magazines in a magazine rack in the customer area for people who are waiting while you finish up their vehicles (current issues only!), and allot a small corner of the waiting room for a coffeemaker or coffee service, a complimentary amenity that will be much appreciated by clients. Just be sure to keep an eye on coffee levels and make a new pot when the brew runs low. Finally, hang a couple of framed prints (of hot cars, of course—or better still, cars you've detailed) and place a potted plant or two in the waiting area to make it look fresh and comfortable, particularly if you're after an upscale clientele. This might be a working garage, but it's style you're after here. Making a good impression on discriminating customers is an important part of doing business.

A sampling of any retail products you sell should be displayed in this area. You can use steel shelving from any home improvement store, but you might consider buying standard retail display racks instead, since they look more professional. Unless you have a clear view into your customer waiting area, you might not want to put a lot of product on the shelves. Easy access can be tempting for someone who can't control the urge to help him- or herself to the products. Instead, keep your overstock in your work area and bring out fresh supplies only when customers are ready to pay for them.

Karen Duncan of Union Park Appearance Care Center in Wilmington, Delaware, took detail shop retailing to a new level—she sold greeting cards in the waiting room of her previous shop. "I used to stock cute cards with cars on them from smaller companies like Blue Mountain," she says. "People waiting for their cars would buy them—even the men. A lot of times they'd spent as much as $10 to $15 at a time. Eventually people started to stop by just to buy cards, so I added car models, mugs, key chains and special-order items like sheepskin covers, and they all did well."

Sign of the Times

The final thing you'll need for your new building will be a large, professional-looking sign that announces to the world that you're in business. It should give the name of your detailing shop in letters that are large enough to be seen from the road. If your primary sign can't be seen from all directions (for instance, if your building is on a corner), you should have a sign on each side of the building where traffic passes. Choose exterior signs that are illuminated from within so they can serve as an advertising vehicle for the business even when you're not open.

> **Tip...**
>
> ## Smart Tip
> Free-standing, on-premises signs are usually attached to or cast in a foundation to keep them from toppling over. To make the structure that holds the sign up more aesthetically pleasing, conceal it with a decorative cover like crushed rock or mulch, or surround it with landscaping.

Signage is one of the more costly start-up expenses, but it's truly worth the price. Just be sure to check with the local zoning commission before erecting a sign, even if you're simply replacing the one that was already on the building. Although there's little doubt you'll be able to put *something* on the front of your building, sign ordinances do change. The last thing you want to do is spend big bucks on a great sign only to find out it's over the size limit or the city fathers don't like the particular shade of puce you've chosen.

Finding
Good Help

Are you looking for new challenges, high adventure, and great excitement in your day-to-day business operations? Then hire a few employees.

Employees are integral to making your detailing business grow and expand into new service areas. They allow you to put more mobile detailing vehicles on the road and more bodies in the shop. But they also can be high maintenance and temperamental while they're helping you achieve greater things in your detailing kingdom.

If you're planning to be a solo operator in your new business venture, you can skip ahead to Chapter 9, which deals with professional development opportunities that can make you a better detailer. But if you think you may need additional help now or in the near future, even if it's only a part-time person to vacuum cars and recondition leather seats while you're tinting windshields, then read on.

Labor Pool

Any person who owns and operates a small business wouldn't hesitate to tell you that one of the most challenging aspects of being a business owner is hiring and retaining good employees. The process of hiring can be daunting if you've never done it before, plus the auto detailing industry seems to experience a higher employee turnover than the average service industry. This might be because the "helper" jobs tend to pay minimum wage, and although these employees might be passionate about cars, they may be more passionate about making 25 cents an hour more at the local quick-lube joint. Also, with the exception of a few training programs and a handful of courses on videotape, there isn't an education track for becoming a detailer like there is for becoming an auto mechanic or a computer technician. As a result, you'll probably find yourself constantly looking for eager, bright, and motivated workers who can be trained in the basic techniques of detailing.

Hiring inexperienced help isn't necessarily a bad thing. Several of the detailers *Entrepreneur* spoke to said they prefer to hire people who *don't* have detailing experience. "It's more difficult to change the habits employees learned elsewhere than it is to teach them how to clean cars my way," says Dave Echnoz of 14/69 Carwash Supercenter in Fort Wayne, Indiana.

Be that as it may, just remember that a lot rides on your employees' skills. Not only are they the frontline representatives of the business, their ability and talent, as well as their attitudes, work ethic, and attention to detail, will influence every aspect of operations, from the client retention rate to the bottom line. For these reasons, you'll want to select your employees very, very carefully.

"I look for the person who has a mind-set to be on time and doesn't think the world owes him a living," says Mike Myers of Gem Auto Appearance Center in Waldorf, Maryland.

Smart Tip

Tip...

It's usually better not to hire family or friends. If they don't work out, you'll have to fire them, and that could create a very uncomfortable situation around the dinner table. The sole exception might be your spouse, who's supposed to love you no matter what. Just don't let your marriage suffer as a result of your business.

"Then I try to instill my own philosophy and teach them what works for me in today's business climate. When it really clicks and someone gets it, it makes you proud."

The Usual Suspects

There are two types of employees you're most likely to need as a new detailer. The first is the detailing technician who will do everything from emptying ashtrays to putting away new shipments of wax and tire dressing. At least initially, you'll want to handle the more difficult tasks yourself. According to Prentice St. Clair of Detail in Progress in San Diego, the average vehicle has at least ten different types of surfaces that need to be maintained, and until you've had a chance to work with a new employee and train him/her on the proper use of equipment and chemicals used for each of these surfaces, don't entrust a customer's car to that person. Period. The technician also can pick up and deliver vehicles to customers' homes and, once trained, can take a mobile van on the road to find work. For this reason, you should make a driver's license and a good driving record conditions of employment for your technicians. Technicians earn anywhere from minimum wage to $10 an hour. Adding incentives for superior work can be an effective way to motivate a good employee to greatness.

The second type of employee you might consider hiring is an assistant manager. Now you're probably thinking, "Whoa, I can hardly pay myself! How can I afford a manager?"

An assistant manager isn't for every detailing business. But if your operation is so successful that you need to hire someone more experienced right away to help with the flotilla of vehicles you detail, then an assistant manager is a good option. In exchange for a title and a little more money than the average technician gets, you'll get someone who can hit the ground rolling, so to speak. In addition to detailing and picking up and delivering vehicles, this person can assist with paperwork, reconcile the cash drawer, make bank deposits, and so on. If possible, look for someone who has worked in an automotive environment because he/she will understand your business and your clientele better. For the extra assistance this person will provide, you should pay $8 to $12 an hour.

Start your search for employees with the right stuff in the advertising section of your local newspaper. Instead of just placing a line ad, which is one of those three- to five-line ads that gets lumped in with all the other help-wanted ads, request an ad with a box around it to make it stand out. If your newspaper has a section devoted to automotive industry jobs—with everything from managers to mechanics—you'll want to place your ad there. You'll find a sample classified ad on page 94.

Be aware that a one-time insertion probably isn't going to be enough to find the right candidate(s). Ask about the newspaper's multiple insertion rate to get the best

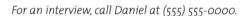

Sample Classified Ad

Automotive Detailer Wanted

Do you love washing and waxing your car until it shines like new?
Then *Great Lakes Automotive Detailing* could have just
the right job for you! As an auto detailer, you'll take care of
all kinds of vehicles, both inside and out. No experience is necessary, although a valid dri-
ver's license and a clean driving
record are a must. We offer competitive wages and paid vacation after
one year.

For an interview, call Daniel at (555) 555-0000.

value for your advertising dollar, and be prepared to run the ad many times to generate enough prospects.

Or you can be like one of Prentice St. Clair's detailing associates and run your ad
continuously. He has four mobile units and keeps his help-wanted ad running all the
time. He treats his search for employees like a normal part of his operation, not a cri-
sis. He just keeps calling the next person on the list.

Web-based job boards like Monster.com or your local newspaper's own internet
classified section are also good places to post a help-wanted ad. If the web site has
enormous reach (as in the case of Monster, which is a national web site), be sure to
include your city and state in the ad so you don't have applicants from Jasper, Indiana,
applying in vain for your $5.25-an-hour detailing job in Walla Walla, Washington.

Back to School

After the newspaper, probably your next richest source of detailing talent will be
found at the local high school or even a community college (especially if it offers training for automotive careers, including auto mechanics). R. L. "Bud" Abraham, president of Detail Plus Car Appearance Systems in Portland, Oregon, recommends
contacting these facilities and arranging to participate in their Career Day events, during which students meet with people from a wide variety of industries to get them
thinking about a future career. "Also, many high schools have work release programs
for vocational studies students who don't plan to attend college," Abraham says. "If
you can formalize a training program of your own, it will serve as a shoo-in to get all
the good candidates you need."

If the students you meet are at least 18 (and can prove it) and are interested in a job, take their names and arrange an interview in person at your shop right away. If you're mobile, ask prospects to meet you at a job site or other neutral location. Even though 16-year-olds may work legally in some parts of the country, you'll probably find they're not mature enough for the job, and, in fact, they may not have enough upper-body strength to handle power tools.

Bright Idea

When prospecting for employees at high school career events, bring informational brochures about your business, a card with your web site address, and some advertising specialty items like pencils imprinted with your business name. Even if the student doesn't come to you for a job, that pencil may get around and spark someone else's interest in your business.

The Little Details

It should go without saying that you want employees who are well-groomed. Since an employee's appearance is a reflection on the capability of your staff and the quality of your services, their appearance should be clean-cut, neat, and professional. (See Chapter 6 for a brief discussion on the merits of having a uniform program.) Long hair on men is fine as long as it's neatly secured away from the face during business hours, if only because it could get caught in the equipment with painful results. As for trendy "bodywear" like multiple piercings and tattoos, if you eliminate any young person who expresses him/herself that way, you may not have any candidates to choose from. As long as such personal expressions of individuality don't detract from the person's detailing ability, they shouldn't be a problem, although if the tattoo is profane, you might want to ask if he/she would mind keeping it covered during business hours.

Finally, it's a plus if the technician is friendly and has a good gift of gab, and patience and careful attention to detail are musts.

Taking the Plunge

Even if you go into a job interview knowing exactly the kind of person you want, the actual hiring process can be a little scary. You may be afraid you'll make a bad decision. You may feel like you're not a very good judge of character, or you won't know what to ask in a job interview. You may be concerned that employees will steal from you or damage your reputation with their sloppy work. You can protect yourself by asking for and checking references, as well as having a 90-day trial period as a condition of employment. During that time, you can evaluate a person's natural aptitude for the work and his/her dependability.

Before a candidate arrives for an interview (either at your facility or at a neutral place like a coffee shop), jot down a list of questions you want to ask, or use the questions found on page 97. You want to ask questions that touch on general topics like the person's background and interests. That's because your candidates are likely to have little or no experience, so you'll want to know about what else he/she has done as a way to gauge that person's suitability for the detailing job. Even if you have a great memory, you should write your questions down, since once the interview gets underway, it can be easy to forget something important you really wanted to ask.

It's also helpful to have a prepared job description that can be given to the candidate. It should include a brief description of the work to be performed, the employee's responsibili-

Beware!
Ground-fault circuit interrupters (GFCIs), which interrupt electrical current to prevent electrocution, are required for electrical circuits installed around water sources, including the area where you wash cars. If your location was built before 1981 (when the National Electrical Code went into effect), you should immediately replace the old outlets with GFCIs.

ties, and the additional support this person is expected to provide (such as answering the phone when the owner is out getting coffee or sweeping up at the end of the day). This is especially important because a lot of people have the mistaken idea that detailing means adding pinstripes or other custom details to a vehicle. You'll want to make it clear that detailing is about restoring and preserving, not customizing.

Every candidate should fill out an official job application, either while waiting in your reception area or at home after the interview. You'll need information like a Social Security number and a mailing address if you hire the person. You can purchase blank application forms at office supply stores, a package of 100 runs about $6. Be sure to shred the applications of any candidates you don't hire, and keep current employees' applications under lock and key to prevent identity theft.

During the interview, outline the job responsibilities and your expectations, then allow the candidate to do most of the talking. As you listen, watch body language. A confident person will sit up straight in the chair and make direct eye contact with you. In addition, someone who is both articulate and friendly will probably be good with customers.

It's quite likely you'll make a decision whether to hire someone at the initial meeting, but it's better to wait until you've checked references. And don't feel compelled to discuss pay and benefits (if any) at this first interview. Wait until you make an offer, either by phone if you're mobile or in person at your facility.

The Benefits of Belonging

It's becoming more common for even the smallest businesses to offer certain benefits to full-time employees as a way to retain them. Health insurance is probably not an option for most detailers because it's so expensive, but offering a perk like one week paid vacation after a year's service or a couple of personal days can make employees

Interview Questions for a Detailing Technician

1. Where did you/do you go to school? _____
_____

2. What's your favorite subject? Why? _____
_____

3. When did you graduate? _____
_____

4. Where did you work previously? _____
_____

5. Do you have any references? May I call them? _____
_____

6. Do you know what an auto detailer does? (An important question—a lot
of people seem to think detailing is the same as customizing.) _____
_____
_____

7. Why do you want to be an auto detailer? _____
_____
_____

8. What do you think is the most important trait a detailer should have
besides the ability to do the job? _____
_____

9. Are you good with people? What makes you think so? _____
_____

10. What would you do if a client wasn't satisfied with a service you provided?
_____
_____

happier and induce them to stick with you, especially if the competition isn't offering similar benefits. Incentives can also be very motivational. For some creative ideas on building employee morale, read "Pump 'Em Up" below.

Taxing Issues

No discussion of employees would be complete without bringing up your obligations to your favorite Uncle Sam. As an employer, you'll be required to withhold several different types of taxes from your employees, including income tax, FICA (aka Social Security), and Medicare. You're also required to keep detailed records about the amount withheld and when it was sent in to the IRS (usually quarterly). Your accountant can help you set up a system for paying federal, state, and local taxes in a timely fashion and recording these tax payments properly. For more information

---

Pump 'Em Up

Whether you have a two-person shop or one with a dozen or more employees, one of your most important duties as team leader is to build employee morale. Human resources experts say that acknowledging and using employees' ideas is crucial for the success of a company, not only because it encourages employee contributions, but also because recognizing their worth makes them feel like an important part of the team. Other ways you can build team spirit include:

○ Expressing appreciation for a job well done (a simple "thank you" or a small token like a $5 gift certificate for a fast-food restaurant can work wonders)

○ Celebrating accomplishments, such as when a new employee learns a new skill, like using a power buffer

○ Allowing employees to borrow company equipment when it's not in use to detail their own cars (with the stipulation that it must be returned in the same condition as it went out)

○ Offering criticism constructively and privately—never in front of customers or other employees

○ Making a reasonable effort to keep jobs interesting

○ Promoting a family atmosphere by hosting enjoyable activities outside work, like a summer barbecue for your employees and their immediate family members

○ Sharing product samples with your employees

○ Providing ear and eye protection, as well as company shirts and hats, at no charge

---

about withholding and taxes, pick up a copy of IRS Publication 15, *Employer's Tax Guide*, as well as Publication 583, *Starting a Business and Keeping Records*. Both are available online from www.irs.gov or at your local IRS office.

And that's not all. The employer incurs a tax liability for every employee. You must pay the matching portion of the FICA tax, which in 2004 was 6.2 percent; and the matching portion of Medicare taxes (1.45 percent). You also must pay state unemployment taxes (to fund payments to employees who are fired or laid off), a self-employment tax (that's the Social Security tax on your personal earnings since you're self-employed), and Federal Unemployment Tax (FUTA), which pays for unemployment insurance programs (another

> ### Smart Tip
>
> Lucky you—the federal government has made paying your business taxes easier with EFTPS-Direct. This free electronic payment method allows you to pay by PC or phone using your employer identification number or Social Security number. You'll also need to provide bank routing information so your account can be debited. For more information or to enroll, call (800) 945-8400, or log on to www.eftps.gov.

6.2 percent). Luckily, you may be eligible to claim a 5.4 percent credit on this amount if you paid state unemployment insurance. Consult with your accountant. Finally, you'll have to pay for workers' compensation insurance, which covers employees' medical expenses and disability benefits if they're injured on the job. The amount varies by state, so contact your state labor department for guidance on how much to set aside.

With all these taxes, it's no wonder some small-business owners pay employees (or themselves) under the table instead of giving Uncle Sam his due. But don't do it. You could find yourself in federal hot water if you're not square with the IRS. And don't think no one will find out that you're not paying taxes. All it takes is one disgruntled customer, one jealous competitor, or even one angry ex-employee to bring the whole house of cars down on your head.

Another way some employers try to evade all this federal folderol is by using independent contractors rather than employees. An independent contractor is a person who's not actually on the payroll even though he or she provides certain services for your business. The problem is, this can be a minefield of potential problems because the IRS has very strict definitions about what constitutes an employee vs. an independent contractor. According to the IRS web site at www.irs.gov, a person is a contractor if "you, the payer, have the right to control or direct only the result of the work done by an independent contractor and not the means and methods of accomplishing the result."

Now here's what the IRS says about employees: "A general rule is that anyone who performs services for you is your employee if you can control what will be done and how it will be done."

Translated, that means if someone works at your facility or if he/she is under your direct supervision while the work is being done, that person is an employee, and you'd better ante up those taxes pronto.

If you're seriously interested in using independent contractors and want to stay on the right side of the law, visit the IRS site to download Publication 15-A, *Employers' Supplemental Tax Guide*, or pick up a copy from your nearest IRS field office.

Workplace Safety Issues

Speaking of government regulations, there's a whole government mandate devoted to workplace safety. The Occupational Safety and Health Act of 1970 (OSHA) has specific requirements that employers must meet to ensure the safety of their workers. These standards are very precise and deal with things like protecting your workers from injury when using hazardous chemicals (basically anything that can be inhaled), protecting them against noise-induced hearing loss, and providing proper ventilation when using flamma-

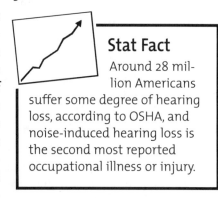

Stat Fact
Around 28 million Americans suffer some degree of hearing loss, according to OSHA, and noise-induced hearing loss is the second most reported occupational illness or injury.

ble and combustible sprays (virtually anything in a spray can). You'll find additional information about OSHA regulations at OSHA's web site at www.osha.gov. Beyond that, be sure to keep work areas free of items like used towels that people can trip over, and immediately clean up spills that can cause a slip-and-fall injury.

9

Owner's Manual
Your Guide to Professional Development

Since automotive detailing is an industry that requires such a high degree of technical ability and skill, you'd think there would be scores of educational and informational resources available to help detailers learn how to ply their craft in the most professional way possible. But surprisingly, that's not the case. There's no such thing as "Detailer

▲

University," as R. L. "Bud" Abraham of Detail Plus Car Appearance Systems in Portland, Oregon, puts it, nor is there even a dedicated professional detailers'association. Instead, a lot of the education is provided by the chemical companies (which, of course, promote only their own products in their seminars); a few detailers or industry experts who have branched out into training; videotape training programs; and the occasional high school program that teaches detailing as an appropriate trade for young people who don't plan to go on to college. Perhaps because of this, a lot of the support in this business comes from among the detailers themselves, who rise above the type of animosity that can be spawned among competitors in any profession and share their ideas and tips. Others like the anonymity of internet chat rooms, where they can wax poetic about products and grouse about problems.

There's a certain amount of frustration among detailers because of this lack of training and information, as evidenced by some of the posts on the detailing bulletin boards. But until someone comes up with the means and a plan to establish a new detailing association to replace the one that folded a few years ago, detailers are pretty much on their own.

This chapter covers the programs, publications, and other sources of information that exist to help detailing professionals do business better, learn new techniques, and grow their business. You'll find contact information for each resource discussed here, as well as many others, in the Appendix.

Industry Associations

While there are many organizations for everything from auto glass to petroleum, detailers have exactly one large-scale association: the International Carwash Association. Located in Chicago, this organization "serve(s) the needs of the carwash and detailing industry's professionals and represent(s) their interests," according to its web site. The organization has been around for 50 years and has more than 3,000 members representing more than 18,000 carwash and detail shop operators. An annual membership is $225.

There are a number of regional carwash associations. You'll find contact information for the larger ones in the Appendix. For a more comprehensive list, visit the International Carwash Association web site at www.carcarecentral.com.

Industry Publications

To stay current on news, information, events, and trends in the detailing industry, you should subscribe to publications that serve both the business owner and his/her clientele. Here's a brief rundown on some of the major publications:

- *Auto Laundry News* covers issues of importance to both carwash owners and detailers. Recent stories of interest to detailers focused on special detailing problems and their solutions as well as detailing the engine compartment. Thirteen issues, including the annual buyer's guide, cost $56. The buyer's guide alone is $15. Published by E.W. Williams Publications Co.

- *Auto Week*, which calls itself America's fastest car magazine, is a weekly consumer magazine that covers vehicle tests, industry news, race coverage, and other cool auto news. A subscription costs $39.95. Published by Crain Communications.

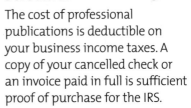
- *Detailer's Digest* costs $15 for six tabloid-sized issues. It's published monthly by Sun King Publishing & Promotions. Get a free trial subscription at http://mobileworks.com/publications.html.

- *Mobile-Tech News & Views* costs $15 for six tabloid-sized issues. It's published monthly by Sun King Publishing & Promotions. Get a free trial subscription at http://mobileworks.com/publications.html.

- *Modern Car Care* is a national trade magazine for the car-care industry that covers business issues of interest to carwash, detail shop, and fast lube operators. A one-year subscription costs $34.50. Published by Virgo Publishing Inc.

- *Motor Trend* is a consumer publication that includes reviews of domestic and foreign cars, comparison tests, race coverage, and new car previews—in short, anything the autophile needs to know. A one-year subscription costs $10. A Primedia Business publication.

- *Professional Carwashing & Detailing* is the official publication of the International Carwash Association (ICA). It covers the vehicle cleaning and detailing industries and their suppliers, with an emphasis on carwash issues. However, detailers will find enough between the covers to make the subscription worthwhile. For instance, a recent issue included articles about attracting high-end detailing customers, creating the perfect detail shop, offering prewax services, and stopping swirl stress. Twelve monthly issues, plus an extra issue in November, cost $59. You can sign up for a free trial subscription at ICA's web site at www.carcarecentral.com. Published by National Trade Publications.

Web Sites, Publications, and Chat Rooms

There's also a slew of free e-zines and detailing web sites in cyberspace that can get your motor racing. Just a few include:

- Automotivedetailing.com: www.automotivedetailing.com, an e-zine
- *Professional Car Care eNews:* www.informz.net/ntp_cw/profile.asp
- *Professional Car Care Online:* www.carwash.com

Sites that offer free detailing newsletters include:

- www.detailking.com
- www.bettercarcare.com

Finally, there are many detailing forums and chat rooms online. Here's just a sampling of what you'll find:

- *Ask the Expert:* a forum sponsored by Detail Plus Car Appearance Systems, www.detailplus.com
- *Autodetailing.com automotive detailing forums:* www.automotivedetailing.com /forum/htm
- *Auto Detailing Secrets of the Experts message board:* www.web-cars.com/detail
- *Detail City auto detail and car-care forum:* www.detailcity.com
- *Meguiar's online discussion forum:* www.meguiarsonline.com
- *Mobileworks.com Auto Detailing Forum:* www.mobileworks.com and www.web-sitetool.box.com/tool/mb/mobileworks
- *Rightlook.com reconditioning forums:* www.automotivedetailing.com/forum.htm

Yearning for Learning

As mentioned previously, there aren't many formal training programs available to aspiring detailers. Thompson Education Direct offers a self-study course that's accredited by the Distance Education and Training Council, and students can earn continuing education units for completing the course. The six-part program covers tools and materials, cleaning techniques for everything from late-model vehicles to classic and antique cars, and business skills needed to start and operate an auto detailing business. Unlimited instructor support is available to guide students through the coursework. Students take an open-book exam at the end of each instruction module, and those who complete and pass the entire course earn a career diploma. The program costs $599 plus shipping, and Thompson offers an affordable tuition plan with zero-percent financing so you can pay as you learn.

Another educational option is the professional hands-on and instructional programs and seminars taught by industry professionals. One of the best-known programs is presented by Portland, Oregon-based Bud Abraham of Detail Plus Car Appearance Systems, whose five-day training program covers management, operation, marketing and advertising, merchandising and pricing, and sales strategies. For $2,500 and expenses, Abraham will travel to your location to conduct the personalized program, and there's

Tip...

Smart Tip
Annual industry conventions are a great place to network and trade tips with others who understand your business and concerns. Be sure to attend the social events as well as the business seminars for a chance to hobnob with other owners.

no limit on the number of people who can attend. You can also get the benefit of Abraham's expertise at one of the detailing seminars he presents in major cities across the United States, which are produced in partnership with *Professional Carwashing & Detailing* magazine. The cost of these seminars is $225.

Other fee-based training seminars are offered by Detail King, Auto Detailing Institute, Rightlook.com, and Appearance Plus Inc. You'll find contact information for all these companies in the Appendix.

> ### Bright Idea
> Home and garden shows are a great place to showcase your talents. Buy a car part from a junkyard, buff out half of it, then put it on display in your booth. You're bound to get a lot of comments and questions from attendees—not to mention requests for your business card and service brochure.

Certification

Alas, this is another area where there aren't many choices. However, the respected International Carwash Association makes up for the lack by offering an express detail services certification as a way to validate your express detail services to your customers. The program comes on CD-ROM and can be completed in one hour, after which you take a certification test. Once you pass it successfully, you'll receive a certificate that can be displayed in your shop. The software can also be used to train your employees in the express detailing process. The program with certification for one person is $159 for ICA members and $295 for nonmembers. Additional employees can be certified for $79 apiece.

Product Seminars

Some of the best free training in this industry is sponsored by the chemical companies. Their motivation may seem self-serving (they want you to buy their products), but they actually are doing a good deed by inviting detailers to learn how to use the products properly. Check the web sites of companies whose products you like to see whether they offer free training.

Trade Shows

Although most of the detailers *Entrepreneur* spoke to didn't carve time out of their busy schedules to attend trade shows, these industry events (which are held at both the national and regional levels) can be very useful for a new detailing business owner. They usually include keynote speakers, educational sessions, and networking opportunities. ICA's Car Care World Expo is considered the industry's premier trade show for professionals, and the Midwest Carwash Association's Expo is one of the industry's largest regional car-care shows. These shows are listed in the Appendix.

Driving the Competition

Are you the type of person who zaps TV commercials before the pitch person utters a single word, shakes subscription cards out of magazines and gleefully stomps on them, and uses the color advertising sections to wrap gifts when you run out of holiday paper? Well, those days are over. Because now that you're gearing up to start your own business, you'll never look at advertising the same way again.

Advertising that's correctly targeted and has a message that grabs attention can be very effective for pulling potential customers into the orbit of your business planet. As Stephen Butler Leacock, a Canadian economist and humorist, put it, "Advertising is the science of arresting the human intelligence long enough to get money from it." As such, its goal is to make people aware of you when you set up shop, then keep them coming back as you become an established member of the business community.

Here are some effective ways a detailer can arrest human intelligence.

Setting the Wheels in Motion

No doubt you'll be happy to know that you don't have to spend a lot to make a big advertising splash. Simple and cost-effective tools like sales letters, fliers, newspaper ads, door hangers, and postcards are often all that's necessary to drum up new business. But you do need a flexible plan for marketing your services to your customers, because scattershot advertising is as bad as no advertising at all.

Your marketing plan doesn't have to be complicated. But it must be in writing, and it has to contain enough information to help you identify market trends and react to seasonal changes, since this helps you determine which types of advertising will be most effective. It also should be flexible so you can alter and update it as market conditions change. This helps you stay in touch with the needs of your customers and continually devise new ways to meet them.

The major components of a marketing plan are the following:

- *Executive summary.* This section summarizes the main points of the entire plan and should be written last, after you've hashed out your overall strategy. At most, the summary will be one page—at least, just a few paragraphs.
- *Objectives.* In this section, you'll discuss what you want to accomplish with your marketing efforts and create a reasonable timetable for achieving your objectives. Putting objectives into writing helps to solidify them in your mind and give you direction. Here are some sample objectives for a new detailer:
  - Earn $10,000 in the first quarter of operation.
  - Seek work from local dealerships to supplement regular business.
  - Learn how to perform new services the competition doesn't offer.
- *Market analysis.* You can use some of the information you included in your business plan for this section. Review the demographics of your market area, then make some assumptions about what types of marketing will work best. For instance, are you situated in a working-class neighborhood? Then couponing might work well. Or are there a lot of urban professionals in the area? Those prospects might respond better to a frequent-buyer program.

- *Marketing strategy.* You've got objectives on paper; now figure out what you have to do to accomplish them and include that info in this section. To illustrate, here's how you can turn the objectives given above into marketing strategies:
  - Earn $10,000 in the first quarter by detailing one car per day at $150 per car (six days a week = 78 days x $150 per car = $11,700).
  - Personally stop by each of the area's auto dealerships to meet the service manager and discuss the detailing services my company offers.
  - Take a course in paintless dent repair to attract customers my competition can't service.
- *Proposed marketing activities.* This is basically a to-do list that includes all the marketing activities you're planning, like putting fliers on cars in the mall parking lot, the period in which you'll do it (pick the actual dates), and who will do the actual work (you, a high school kid you hire to slip fliers under windshield wipers, etc.). Try putting this information into a spreadsheet program like Excel or even on an accountant's pad so you can see exactly what you're planning and when it's supposed to happen.
- *Budget.* In this section, you'll make some assumptions about where you'll spend your dollars, like on those fliers mentioned above or door hangers (those coated paper tags that are hung on prospective customers' front doors).
- *Performance tracking.* Establishing some benchmarks you can measure your marketing efforts against helps you figure out whether they're working and whether they're worth doing again.

You'll find some additional information about writing marketing plans at the SBA's web site at www.sba.gov.

Did you notice that many of the items in your marketing plan are similar to those in your business plan? That's done deliberately. The difference is that your business plan gives the big picture, while your marketing plan is a more narrow view. Both are important to keeping the business on track as well as for obtaining financing. Lenders will be so impressed by your shrewd business sense and entrepreneurial spirit that they won't be able to write you that start-up check fast enough.

Shifting into High Gear

Just when you thought you'd done all the planning you could possibly stand, we have to break the news to you that you still have to plan your actual promotional strategy. First off, set a budget. A good rule of thumb is to set your budget as a percentage of projected gross sales. A budget of 2 to 5 percent is a modest yet reasonable amount for a start-up business.

So let's say you're projecting gross sales of $50,000 in your inaugural year. Using the 2 to 5 percent rule, that works out to an advertising budget of $1,000 to $2,500 a year. Luckily, most of the advertising tools that are most effective for detailers are pretty inexpensive—like a mere $25 for 500 fliers printed for 5 cents each at Kinko's or around $375 for 2,500 postcards, plus postage. (If you're not going to use all 2,500 in a single mailing, make sure they're generic enough so you can use them for a subsequent mailing.) So even a modest advertising budget can go a long way.

> **Bright Idea**
>
> Advertising specialty items imprinted with your business name and hone number are an inexpensive way to advertise. Buy items that people will use, like pens, key chains, and even squeeze water bottles, then pass them around freely. Or leave them on the dashboard with a thank-you note after finishing the job.

As part of your start-up costs, you should include a larger sum of cash for initial promotional and marketing costs. You'll want to make a grand splash to let your public know you're out there. A budget of $1,000 to $2,000 should be enough to cover the survey work we mentioned in Chapter 3, newspaper ads, promotional fliers, and if you're working out of a fixed location, maybe even a modest grand opening event, which you'd also want to advertise. At this event (which might run from 11 A.M. to 2 P.M. on a Saturday), you could show off some of the vehicles you've meticulously detailed (offer a small honorarium to the owner—say, $50—for the privilege of displaying his or her vehicle), and provide snack food or serve something simple like hot dogs, potato chips, and soft drinks to induce people to stick around and look over the vehicles on display.

Next, decide what kinds of ongoing advertising you'd like to do, and create a written schedule that details exactly when you'll make it happen. A new business should advertise pretty much all the time as a way to build up clientele. While the trick is to figure out which methods will work best in your market, the types of advertising that tend to work best for detailers are postcards, fliers, door hangers, newspaper ads, and Yellow Pages ads.

Card 'Em

Postcards are an inexpensive way to reach a lot of people. They don't require an envelope, they qualify for a reduced postage rate, and they can easily be created using the Postcard Wizard in Microsoft Word. All you do is type in the text, and the wizard does all the formatting. Just make sure the text is grammatically correct and error-free. You'll hurt your credibility as a careful and competent detailer by sending out a postcard that says you're "Noe open for business" or that you offer a discount to people who refer their "fiends." To save even more money, you can print them on your home computer, but by the time you factor in the time you'll spend feeding card stock through the auxiliary paper handler and the amount you'll spend on the materials, it may actually be more cost-effective to have them printed for you. You'll find some printing resources in the Appendix.

As you'll recall from Chapter 3, you don't have to compile your own mailing list; you simply buy a targeted mailing list. Ask for the outputted list on pressure-sensitive labels, slap 'em on the cards while you're chilling out in front of the TV, and mail 'em. Then wait for the business to pour in.

Dollar Stretcher

Get more bang for your buck by advertising on your local cable TV system. Since cable stations usually reach a fairly small regional area, a "bulletin board" ad will be see by precisely the people you're trying to reach. Call the cable system's sales department for advertising rates before you pay to produce an ad.

"Advertising is good for generating high-volume work, like basic washing and waxing," says Prentice St. Clair, the San Diego detailer and industry expert. "It helps you appeal to a larger percentage of the population."

You can use postcards to announce your arrival in the business community, to introduce new services, to announce a sale on retail products you carry, and so on.

Paper Promotions

Speaking of advertising on the cheap, you can't beat fliers and advertising door hangers. Fliers are simple to create on your home computer. They're generally one-sided, on 8.5-by-11-inch paper, so they can be folded to fit a standard No. 10 envelope or tucked under a windshield wiper wherever cars are parked. Word has a flier template you can use to mock up your own flier, plus you'll find a sample you can use as inspiration on page 112.

Although fliers are cheap, they, too, have to be professional-looking and free of errors. "My partner and I made [our first] fliers on my kitchen table," says Anthony Orosco, owner of Ultimate Reflections in San Antonio. "They were horrible, and we didn't get one call from them. We invested some money in our next fliers, and the very afternoon we handed them out, we received a call from a business to detail a Lexus and two Mercedes. So let that be a lesson to all you aspiring detailing entrepreneurs: Don't skimp on your image! Go to the professionals for your business cards and fliers."

Often, the quickie printers like American Speedy Printing can help you design a nice flier at little expense. Alternatively, you can find a graphic designer in the Yellow Pages who will do the job for about $100.

Door hangers cost a little more but deliver a lot of look for the money. The standard size is 4-by-9 inches, and there's a hole cut at the top (known as a die cut) so they can be hung on every doorknob you can find. They're usually printed in full color on

Make your vehicle look showroom new again!

Spring special—Complete auto detailing just $175**

Price includes:

Hand wash and dry
Interior cleaning and reconditioning
(including carpets, upholstery, vinyl/leather)
Exterior buff and wax
Windows, tire/wheel cleaning, and more

Offer expires May 31

For an appointment, call

Great Lakes Automotive Detailing

5555 Jefferson Ave.
St. Clair Shores, Michigan 48051
(555) 555-0000
www.greatlakesdetailing.com
info@greatlakesdetailing.com

Pick up and delivery service available
Visa, MasterCard, and American Express accepted

*Average-sized vehicle. Price may vary depending on size/condition of vehicle.

heavy paper that has a UV coating to prevent fading from the sun or inclement weather. One company we researched charges $444 (or 8.8 cents each) for 5,000 hangers. (This assumes that you use one of the company's templates; if you design the hanger yourself, it will cost you more.) If you make the copy generic enough (for instance, avoid promoting a special sale or other dated event), the initial quantity will give you enough to blanket your target area several times. You'll find the names of a few companies that print door hangers in the Appendix under the "Printing Resources" heading. Before you go out and do the deed, however, check with the city you'll be working in to see whether a solicitor's license is needed to distribute door hangers. The cost is likely to be nominal ($10 or so), and having a license will keep you out of trouble in case one of the neighbors complains to the police.

Brochures are useful for a variety of purposes. Format them to fit a No. 10 envelope, and you can use them for direct-mail advertising. You can also display them in a holder on your service counter (or hand them to your mobile customers) as a way to explain those lucrative add-on services you offer, like paintless dent repair, black trim recoating, leather treatment, and so on. You can also enclose them with a sales letter (see sample on page 114) sent to a selected mailing list with the intention that the prospect will read the letter when it arrives, then save the brochure for future reference.

To save money on the brochure design, you can use the Word brochure template. Just keep in mind that graphic design takes skill and creativity, and a do-it-yourself version might not project the image you're looking for. Consider hiring a professional to do the job. If that's beyond your budget, call the art department at your local community college or university and ask someone in the fine arts department to refer you to a talented student, who will charge you *much* less than a professional designer.

As for the copy, make sure your brochure includes your phone number, your brick-and-mortar address or post office box, and your web site and/or e-mail address prominently. It's also a great idea to enclose a business card with any mailing piece that goes in an envelope because people are more apt to file a business card for future reference than a brochure. To get them to open the envelope in the first place, try some of these tricks used by direct-mail pros:

- Use only a return address on the outer envelope to give it the appearance of personal correspondence.
- Use postage stamps rather than a bulk postage indicia, which is a dead giveaway that the envelope contains advertising material.
- Use a teaser line on the outside to induce the recipient to open the envelope. Teasers that incorporate the word "free" (as in "free estimate" or "Buy one service, get one free") or terms like "limited time offer" are powerful motivators.

Cooperative mail packages (aka marriage mail) like the Valpak also can be quite effective for detailers—if you're willing to offer a discount. They consist of numerous advertising fliers or coupons from a variety of different advertisers that are mailed to

Sample Sales Letter

Dear Neighbor:

Before you know it, winter will be here again, along with frigid temperatures, overcast days, and nerve-wracking commutes home in the snow and ice. It's also the time of year that's the hardest on your vehicle. Road salt can eat away at your car, truck, or SUV, damaging its showroom finish, and dirt from the spray of slushy water can penetrate every crevice, from the wheel wells to the side-view mirrors.

Great Lakes Automotive Detailing can help protect your vehicle and minimize winter damage by prepping it for the rough weather ahead. In addition to washing your vehicle with meticulous care, we will hand-wax your car to give it the best possible protection against the elements. We'll make your interior look like new again. We can even remove tough odors and pet stains.

So before Old Man Winter makes an unwelcome return appearance, call the professionals at Great Lakes Automotive Detailing at (555) 555-0000, or visit our web site at www.greatlakesdetailing.com. We'll put a shine on your car, truck, or SUV that will put that lazy old winter sun to shame.

Very truly yours,

Daniel Wayne

Daniel Wayne
Owner
Great Lakes Automotive Detailing

5555 Jefferson Ave. • St. Clair Shores, Michigan 48051 • (555) 555-0000
www.greatlakesdetailing.com • info@greatlakesdetailing.com

every residential and/or business address in a specific area. The fliers usually are sized to fit a No. 10 or a 9.5-by-5.5-inch envelope and may be printed in full color on glossy paper. The cost is usually quite low because your flier rides along with those from a lot of other paying customers. But the disadvantage is that your flier will be "ganged" with others from diverse companies like oil change companies, nail salons, window installers, dentists, and, possibly, other detailers. But the low cost may outweigh any perceived disadvantages.

"Valpak appeals to the cost-conscious customer, which is good if you're interested in doing high-volume detailing," says Prentice St. Clair of Detail in Progress. "Plus, you'll get a lot of phone calls but not necessarily a lot of work."

A little while ago we mentioned that you should send a business card with every direct-mail piece you send out. But your card also can be used as a mini-advertising tool every day. Always keep some in a little holder on your reception desk if you have a facility or in your vehicle if you're mobile (just be sure to keep them clean and dry). You should also look into the possibility of putting a supply of your cards on the counters of companies that might be able to send business your way. Some obvious places include new- or used-car dealerships, quick-lube or express oil-change companies, bump shops, and auto supply stores. Obviously, you should check first to see whether any of them have their own in-house detailing shop.

Business cards are really cheap—so cheap it's not worth your time to do them on your home computer and printer. You'll pay only about $35 for 1,000 cards at national office supply stores like Office Max. If you hold any certifications from detailing product manufacturers or chemical companies, you might want to include that information on your card because it gives you credibility.

Power of the Press

Newspaper advertising can be another effective advertising medium for detailers, particularly when you're starting your business and need visibility fast. Community newspapers and free weekly shoppers offer the most value for your advertising buck, even though they're not published as often as the big city dailies. But even the weekly or monthly papers can pack quite an advertising punch because they're delivered right in the community where you do business. If the paper is free, so much the better, because that means advertising is footing the publication bill, and as a result, every single household will receive a copy.

Tip...

Smart Tip

Before you spend your hard-earned cash on an advertising buy, request a media kit from the medium's ad representative. Media kits contain information that will help you decide whether the publication is right for you, including facts about its editorial content and readership demographics. It will also contain ad rates and an audited circulation statement.

Ads are sold in sizes as small one-eighth of a page and cost less the more times you run them. (Running an ad just once or twice is a waste of your money—you have to be a regular advertiser to get the full benefit of your advertising dollars.) For information about advertising rates and assistance with creating your ads, call the newspaper's outside sales department. If you are creative and would like to design the ad yourself, you can use desktop publishing software like Microsoft Publisher to do the job. To get your creative juices racing, you'll find a sample newspaper ad below.

Bright Idea

Always test the effectiveness of your advertising so you're using your ad dollars wisely. One way to do this is to run the same ad with a coupon in two newspapers but include a different identifying mark in each one. When customers bring in the coupons, you can count how many you got from each newspaper and know which ad pulled better.

If you specialize in detailing high-end vehicles, including high-performance and vintage automobiles, you might consider advertising in a city magazine. But beware: These types of publications tend to be expensive. A better place for your ad might be a regional collector car or car club publication. Check the internet to see what's out there.

Finally, a couple of really inexpensive advertising media are high school newspapers and event programs (like those for student theatrical productions), as well as the backs of grocery store cash register receipts. Offer a coupon with a nominal discount, and watch your business grow.

Sample Newspaper Ad

Make Your Wheels Look Like New Again!
Professional auto detailing

- Cars/trucks/SUVs/vans
- Hand wash/wax/buffing/polishing
- Seat/upholstery cleaning/reconditioning/repair
- Interior/exterior detail packages
- Paintless dent repair/touch-up
- Odor removal/deodorizing
- Engine detailing
- Same day service
- Pick up and delivery available
- Lease turn-in specialist

Great Lakes Automotive Detailing

(555) 555-0000
5555 Jefferson Avenue
St. Clair Shores, MI 48051

All Booked Up

Anyone who has a business phone number automatically gets a basic line ad in the Yellow Pages, which gives your business name, address, and phone number. But the question is, Should you spring for one of the larger display ads (the ones that are boxed and sometimes have spot color) as a way to make your business stand out? To decide, open your local phone book and take a look at the "Automobile Detailing" listings. Are there many display ads? If your book is anything like the SBC East Area Metropolitan Detroit Smart Yellow Pages, then probably not. Of the 41 listings in that directory, only four are true display ads with graphics like photos or clip art. There also are seven one-column-wide, multiline listings with larger type and boxes around them. Just one of those boxed ads includes art of a car. Do the larger ads stand out when you open the book? Definitely. Is it worth the price? Maybe not.

"People who open the Yellow Pages have already made a decision to buy," says Barbara Koch, author of *Profitable Yellow Pages* (FTD Association). "But that's also what makes it unnecessary to buy a display ad in most cases. The real role of your ad is to get customers to choose you over someone else, and factors like your location may be what actually cause them to call you."

Ultimately, your decision to buy a display ad may be based strictly on cost. Display ads usually cost hundreds of dollars a month, and you're locked into an ironclad

Smart Tip

If your phone directory listing can accommodate your web site or e-mail address along with your brick-and-mortar or mobile address, add the information, no matter the cost. A lot of people like to check a company's web site before calling for an appointment, so put the information right up front to make it as easy as possible for them to find you

Radio Rewards

Dave Echnoz of 14/69 Carwash Supercenter in Fort Wayne, Indiana, has figured out the perfect way to get radio airtime without spending a fortune: He worked out a deal with a popular local station to get the DJs to do testimonials on the air. Here's how it works: The DJ casually works in references to the detailing business as part of the on-air chatter, as in "Hasn't the weather been terrible? My car really looks bad after all this snow, so I'm going to get it detailed over at 14/69 Carwash Supercenter this afternoon. They do a really great job." Echnoz says the testimonials don't sound like commercials, and best of all, he pays just $1,000 for 20 of these sound bites.

12-month contract. The good news is that it's possible to include a lot of detail in the ad, like photographs and maps, but of course that drives the price up. It might be better to pay for an extra line for your web site address and let prospects browse your site instead of looking at a photo that will be too small to make much of a difference anyway. We'll talk about web sites and other internet considerations in the next chapter.

Before we move on, here's one more reason you might want a display ad: According to a Yellow Pages Integrated Media Association usage study, three auto-related categories were among the top ten most-referenced headings in 2002, "Automobile Parts-New & Used," "Automobile Repairing & Service," and "Automobile Dealers-New & Used" had 561.1 million, 518.1 million, and 284.9 million hits, respectively. The used-car listings come right before the auto detailing listings in the SBC phone book, which means anyone looking at the new and used listings might see your ad, too.

Talking Up Your Talents

We can't conclude this discussion of advertising techniques without touching on the single most powerful form of advertising available—and one that's absolutely free of charge. We're talking, of course, about word-of-mouth (WOM). It's by far the best way to generate positive buzz about your detailing business, not only because it's cost-effective but also because other people do all the work *for* you. All you have to do is detail your little heart out in the most competent, professional way possible, and your satisfied customers will tell others about you.

Or you can show them what you can do. Gary Kouba of Perfect Auto Finish in Roselle,

Beware!
Experts say that dissatisfied customers often won't say anything to a service provider when they have a bad experience, but they will tell six to seven people about it. Head off that kind of bad publicity by doing whatever it takes to make amends if you suspect a customer isn't happy.

Illinois, wanted to work on high-end cars when he started his business, so he scouted around and found the largest distributor of Lamborghinis, Ferraris, and Lotuses in the Midwest practically in his backyard—a "field of dreams of cars," as he puts it. Kouba offered to detail a car at no charge to show the dealer what he could do, and the dealer liked his work so much that he now delivers a car to the detailer in an enclosed trailer every other day—cars with sticker prices of up to $285,000.

There are other ways to generate positive WOM yourself. Try these techniques:

- Call your clients shortly after completing the job to ask for feedback and verify that they're satisfied. Not only will they be shocked that you called (since it's very rare for businesspeople in service industries to follow up after the sale), but they'll be impressed that you cared enough to call—and they're likely to tell others about the experience.

- Leave a thank you note and a small gift—say a bottle of vinyl dressing, a $5 gift certificate for the local coffee bar, or a long-stemmed rose—on the front seat where the customer will find it.

- Offer a referral reward to clients who refer their friends and family. The reward can be modest—say, 25 percent off a full detailing. Not only does this increase business, but it makes salespeople out of your own customers.

Stat Fact

According to a survey by Attard Communications, up to 54 percent of small businesses report they land most of their clients through networking, referrals, and word-of-mouth advertising.

- Donate time doing something positive and visible in your community. For example, you could hold a free detailing seminar for high school seniors who are interested in automotive-related trades. We'll tell you how to get free publicity for this type of event in Chapter 12.

Internet Marketing
and Research

Imagine having an enthusiastic, totally committed salesperson on your staff who labors for you night and day no matter what the weather, who isn't affected by the flu season, warm summer days, or high school football practice, and who doesn't ask for comp time. Well, you may already have Robo Employee on your staff. It's called the World Wide Web.

▲

Besides revolutionizing the way people shop, do business (think online checking and Internet shopping), and fritter away their leisure time in chat rooms, the internet has a very real business function: It can direct new customers to you and help you find practically any information you need to do business better. This, of course, is what makes the internet an invaluable tool for detailers. Even if you never answer a single e-mail query about special services you offer, you still need to have a web site. People are now used to having information available when they want it—whether it's 3 P.M. or 3 A.M. Your Yellow Pages ad can only give so much information. Your web site can give so much more.

Statistics confirm the power of the internet. Results of a 2003 Harris Poll showed that 67 percent of all adult Americans were online. They surf from home, work, libraries, cyber cafes, and other locations, and many of them access the web from two or more places. So if a guy is showing off his freshly detailed hot rod at lunch, his coworkers can go online right away to find someone to make a shrine out of their vehicles, too. Plus, they can do it whenever it's most convenient, including during business hours if the boss isn't around.

In addition to accessibility, there are many other advantages to having a web site. First, it gives you more visibility for very little cost. It allows you to post a comprehensive list of your services and prices so you and your staff can spend your time buffing and polishing rather than yakking on the phone, running though a litany of your offerings. It can even schedule appointments (if you have the right software) or automatically send out e-newsletters advertising specials and product sales to your valued customers or prospects.

For the purposes of this chapter, we'll assume you have at least a general knowledge of the internet, including knowing how to log on to an ISP, use a search engine, and send and retrieve e-mail. But if you haven't had much experience with this powerful medium, you should learn how to use it immediately. Virtually every community college and adult education program, and possibly your local public library, offers courses that can acquaint you with the basics of surfing the web. There are also many books (like the "Dummies" series books) and software packages available that can guide you through the process.

Your Own Cyber Space

The proliferation of web sites over the past few years has driven the cost of creating, hosting, and maintaining them way down to the point where anyone can afford them—even your niece in fourth grade, whose site consists of digital photos of her tabby kitten. Many ISPs provide their subscribers with a certain amount of free web page space—say, 10MB. This is sufficient if all you want to post is an electronic "business card," or a static site that doesn't allow navigation. This kind of site is useful for posting hours, telephone numbers, and other information customers might need when the shop isn't open. But to have a really great site, you have to be able to post useful information and change it periodically to give it a fresh, new look. That means you're going to have to pay for web page hosting, which fortunately starts for as little as $4.95 a year. (To find a host of web hosts, type "web hosting" into your browser.)

Here are some elements you should consider having on your web page:

- *Services and packages.* This is the info people will most commonly be after when they visit your site. So you'll want to describe in detail every service and package you offer. This serves two purposes. As mentioned earlier, it keeps you from spending a lot of time on the phone describing your services to prospects. It also allows you to upsell, or suggest other services the customer might be interested in.

  There are varying opinions on whether or not prices should be posted on a web site where anyone (including your competition) can see them. But industry experts and detailers alike agree that showing your prices upfront is more helpful than not.

- *Flash intro.* If you've ever logged on to a web page and had a grizzly bear rear up and growl at you or saw a NASCAR performance car roar across the screen, then you know what Flash is. Although Flash intros are used to grab attention, they take a while to load and play, and people can be impatient to get through the intro and into the site they're visiting. If you decide to use Flash, be sure to place a "skip intro" option on the Flash page so eager readers can bypass your artwork and get to the point. Your Flash intro also shouldn't be too long for the same reason. Hook 'em with cool graphics; don't lull them to sleep (or tempt them to click ahead to someone else's site). A good length to shoot for might be five seconds.

  Naturally, after the Flash intro, the user should be taken to a navigation page, which will have links to some of the elements discussed below. This navigation page also should have full contact info, including your detailing shop name, address, phone number, and even your web address and e-mail address because a lot of people print home pages for future reference or as a reminder to call for more information later. For that matter, your contact info should be on every page of your site, even if it's in "mouse type" (six-point type or less) along the very bottom of each page. Also use dark type that's easy to read. Neon orange may look really cool on the screen, but it could wash out completely when printed.

  If you have one, you can also use your logo on each page of your web site. A logo is a visual symbol that represents your company. Examples include the Ford blue oval (with Henry Ford's own signature) and Microsoft's butterfly emblem. If you're creative, you can

> **Tip...**
>
> **Smart Tip**
> If you want to sell detailing products online, you'll need a business hosting service rather than a standard web host. The premium price you'll pay covers the extra storage space as well as maintenance and upgrades on the site.

fashion your own logo using a graphics program like the Logo Creator by Laughingbird Software ($69.95).

- *Portfolio.* There's no better way to demonstrate auto detailing skill than by posting photos of vehicles you've painstakingly detailed. Your photo gallery should include both interior and exterior shots to show off your abilities. Posting before-and-after photos like Anthony Orosco of San Antonio did on his web site is also a great way to convince prospective clients that you know your stuff.

Stat Fact

A 2002 Harris Interactive poll indicated that 137 million adult Americans (66 percent) are now online. Of these users, 32 percent are college graduates and 46 percent have household incomes above $50,000. The heaviest users are adults age 18 to 39, who make up 51 percent of the cyber population.

"I see [my web site] like an online professional portfolio that I can send to others so they can see my 'art,' " says Orosco, whose web address is www.ultimatereflections.com. "I see a car as a canvas, and the tools and products I use on it are my medium, so my web site is a place where others can go and learn about who I am and what I do."

Your photos don't have to be professional-quality, but they should be taken with a good camera. Try to take the photos in bright sun (although not at noon when the sun is directly overhead), and make sure they're clear and the subject is level. Don't use special effects—your detailing work should speak for itself.

Regular photos must be scanned into your computer, then downloaded to your web site. If you don't have a scanner, you can take the prints to a speedy copy shop and they'll output the photo for you. Better still, invest in a digital camera so you can take photos that can be instantly downloaded to your web site. You can pick up a good starter camera for less than $200. You'll also need a media card reader so you can download the photos to your computer instead of peering at the tiny window on your camera to preview the photos. A media card reader is like another drive for your computer and plugs into the USB port. You simply insert the media card, go to the reader's drive to bring up your photos, and import them into an editing program like MS Photo Editor. Then you can enlarge them, adjust the contrast if you wish, save them to a CD, or download them onto your web page. A card reader costs only about $20.

Keeping in Touch

As mentioned previously, the internet offers a wealth of information for detailers. You can browse product suppliers' online catalogs, learn useful detailing techniques, and get the goods about trade shows coming to your town to judge whether you should attend or reserve booth space. You also can log on to one of the many detailing chat rooms and bulletin boards, where new and established detailers alike congregate in cyberspace to commiserate about challenges and crow about successes.

Stat Fact

Online retail sales in America totaled $45.5 billion in 2002, according to the U.S. Department of Commerce. And the future looks very bright. Jupiter Research estimates online retail spending will reach $105 billion by 2007.

You can get an idea of the scope of information available on the internet by typing "auto detailing" into your browser. A recent search of Google turned up 524,000 sites. "Auto detailing association" yielded 82,500 sites, while "detailing products" resulted in 833,000 sites. Of course, it will take some time to comb through all the sites that pop up (many of which may have no bearing on your search) to find out which ones suit your needs, but chances are it will be easier and faster to surf for what you need than it would be to make phone calls or pore through directories and reference books. Important tip: Limit your search by using more words so fewer sites pop up. For instance, "auto detailing polishing products" will yield far fewer sites than "detailing products."

One really easy way to get information about what's new and exciting in the industry—as well as to commiserate with other owners—is to log on to a detailing industry-related online discussion forum. We've listed just a few in the Appendix, but you'll find there are many more out there. You also can post bulletins on detailing message boards to find useful information, including leads to people selling used orbital sanders—or even an entire detail shop.

You'll also find many sites that offer help with the myriad issues small-business owners face. One place to start is the SBA's site at www.sba.gov, where you'll find information like business management tips and financing options. Related to the SBA's site is www.score.org, a small-business mentoring site that can connect you to a local Service Corps of Retired Executives (SCORE) office in your vicinity. And, of course, you'll want to check out *Entrepreneur* magazine's site at www.entrepreneur.com for everything you ever wanted to know about running a small business.

The best thing about the information you can gather on the internet is that much of it is available to you at no charge other than the cost of the phone call that connects you to the web (if you're still using dial-up). But beware: There are virtually no restrictions when it comes to posting web site or bulletin board messages, so pick your sources carefully. Make sure you're on a reputable web site.

Still another invaluable function of the internet is its communication capabilities. You can order supplies in the dead of night, then stay in touch with suppliers to find out when the polishes and waxes will arrive. Or you can develop your own e-mail list, then use it to keep in touch with your clients and hopefully spur them to come in for touch-up or additional services.

Incidentally, it is now so *uncool* to tie up a phone line when surfing the web. Get a second line if you are surfing in your shop, or sign up for a DSL or digital cable connection.

Building Your Site

In Chapter 5, we recommended hiring a team of professionals to help run your business behind the scenes. Another person you should consider adding to the team on a short-term basis is a web page developer.

A developer will do the programming work necessary to make your site look cool (remember that racing car zooming across the page?) and make all the parts work together. Among other things, he/she will design the site's overall look, invent the flash intro, create links to lead viewers from one screen to the next (in essence creating a multipage online brochure), and implement tools like site counters, if you want them. He/she also can set the site up so you can update it yourself or add new content easily.

A web developer will charge anywhere from $1,000 to $4,000 for a fully functional web site with links. Part of this cost is based on the number of pages on the site. The more complex the site is, the more it costs. Future maintenance and/or updates are usually charged on an hourly basis if you're not doing them yourself. You can find web designers in the Yellow Pages or through your local chamber of commerce or other business organizations.

Gary Kouba of Perfect Auto Finish in Roselle, Illinois, hired a student studying information technology at the local junior college to design his web site. The student created the site as an extra credit assignment, and Kouba paid him just $1,000 for what turned out to be a very professional job.

If you're computer-savvy, you could try creating your own web page by using one of the many web page programs on the market, like Dreamweaver MX by Macromedia (retails for $399, www.macromedia.com) or Microsoft FrontPage (retails for $199, available from CompUSA (www.compusa.com) and Amazon (www.amazon.com).

Copy on the site should be kept brief enough so each topic fits on one page because many people find it annoying to have to keep scrolling down as they read. Other items to include are a coupon to attract new customers (offer a small discount, say, 10 percent, to people who mention your web site) and a list of the various services and packages you offer, with detailed descriptions and prices. Since customers can call and get the same information, you can save them the phone call and your employees the trouble of responding to it by including this information on your web site.

> ### Smart Tip
> *Tip...*
>
> Web site type in colors like yellow can be very difficult to read against a light background. By the same token, don't use colors like royal blue on a black background. If you want your message to come through loud and clear, use black type on a white background. You can't go wrong.

Hosting Duties

You're now close to getting your site up and running. The next step is to select a unique name, known as a domain name (or URL, for Universal Resource Locator). Most detailers use their business name as their domain name if no one else is already using the name. (That could happen with a common name like "Bill's Auto Detailing," which would have a domain name of www.billsautodetailing.com).

Domain names are registered for a minimum of two years and are renewable. The cost to register a name for two years is approximately $70. There are several companies that handle registration, but one of the best known is DOMAIN.com, which also allows you to register your name for five- or ten-year periods. The cost for these longer registrations is $25 and $20 per year, respectively.

Finally, you'll have to select an internet host. Examples of well-known internet hosts include EarthLink and NetPass, but there are many smaller (and gargantuan) hosts around. Just be sure to check the host's rep before signing on. A host that's well-established or that has been in business for a while is your best bet so it doesn't go belly-up one day.

Web hosting is only about $19.95 per month for 20MB of disk space. Some of the hosts also allow you to register your domain at the same time. Web hosting is very competitive, so shop around for the best deal. You can start with the host names you'll find in the Appendix at the end of this book.

Dollar Stretcher

If you decide to use a professional web designer to create your site, consider bartering for his/her services to keep the cost down. While it's unlikely you'll be able to barter for the entire cost of a $4,000 web site, you could offer to give the designer a certain number of detailing services and a cash payment in exchange for the work.

Tooting Your Own Horn

When you were younger, did your mom or some other authority figure (like maybe Sister Mary Assumpta in the sixth grade) tell you that it was better to be seen and not heard, that nice boys and girls don't boast, and that good things come to those who wait?

It's time to forget all that advice. Successful entrepreneurs have to be masters at shameless self-promotion. Oh, you can buy advertising to spread the word about the great service you offer and the outstanding detailing skills you possess. But, as you know, advertising costs money—and that's something you may not have mountains of in the early days of your entrepreneurial venture.

So take a tip from experienced promoters and incorporate low- or no-cost marketing and public relations tools like news releases, newsletters, feature articles, networking, and public speaking engagements into your promotional mix. Here's a rundown of how each one can generate the positive publicity you need.

News Releases

News releases (aka press releases) are like little ads for your business—but in print they look like legitimate news stories. Better still, you don't have to pay for them. Rather, newspapers and magazines use them to fill odd-sized spaces as the need arises. That means, of course, that not every news release you write will get into print. But that's OK, because even if they're not printed, they're valuable because they bring you and your business to the attention of the person who ultimately decides what goes into the publication.

You might be surprised by exactly how much news you'll have to pass on to editors. You can write a release about opening your business, adding new services or product lines, and hiring employees. You can also write about your detail packages and seasonal specials, interesting jobs you've undertaken (like detailing your first yacht), and the humanitarian work you do (like donating a detailing package for a charity auction). The news doesn't have to be earthshaking—just interesting to a general audience.

A news release is usually one page long and gives enough information to pique an editor's interest. When writing the release, answer the basic questions of who, what, where, when, why, and how, and be sure to provide contact information so the editor can reach you if necessary. You'll find a sample news release on page 131 that you can use as a guide. Please note that formatting elements like "For immediate release" are standard for new releases, so you'll want to use them on yours, too.

The chances that your releases will be published in a community paper are pretty good, particularly in business sections that focus on local companies. But you also should send your releases to the big city papers and the other big players in your market (including cable TV and radio), since it's always possible that an editor might be interested enough in some aspect of your detailing business to interview you for a feature story.

You don't have to be a journalist to write a release as long as your basic writing skills are sound. If you prefer, you can use a freelance public relations writer, who will charge $25 to $150 for a one-page news release. You can find freelance writers

Sample News Release

NEWS RELEASE

For immediate release

Date: September 4, 200x
Media contact: Daniel Wayne
Telephone: (555) 555-0000

FALL AUTO MAINTENANCE KEEPS VEHICLES LOOKING GOOD, PROTECTS THEM AGAINST WINTER DAMAGE

ST. CLAIR SHORES, MI—Neither rain nor sleet nor gloom of night can keep vehicles off the streets of metro Detroit. But the elements can take a toll on your vehicle's finish and appearance. That's why the auto reconditioning and restoration experts at Great Lakes Automotive Detailing recommend having your vehicle detailed both inside and out before the snow flies.

"Winter weather is really hard on vehicles around here," says Great Lakes Automotive Detailing owner Daniel Wayne. "Road salt can eat away at a car's finish, while dirt and slush can work their way into every crack and crevice, and will leave a film on windows that can impair a driver's vision."

Washing your car regularly is a great way to ward off damaging salt deposits and keep windows, headlights, and taillights clear. But a complete detailing done in the fall is the best way to protect your vehicle against the worst that winter can dish out.

In addition to hand washing, buffing, and waxing your vehicle, the pros at Great Lakes Automotive Detailing will steam-clean the seats, carpets, and mats; condition the vinyl and leather surfaces; and apply protective dressings to your wheels, tires, and other surfaces. They can also clean the engine compartment and trunk, repair dents, and perform other services to make your vehicle look like new again, while helping it weather a harsh Michigan winter.

For more information about auto detailing or for an appointment, call Great Lakes Automotive Detailing at (555) 555-0000.

through the Yellow Pages, local professional advertising organizations, the chamber of commerce, and university journalism departments.

Newsletters

Newsletters are about the hottest little promotional gimmick around these days. Even though just about every businessperson, from duct cleaners to welders, is publishing a newsletter, they're still a good medium for spreading the word about your particular business niche. That's because they're easy to create, inexpensive to produce, and really effective for delivering targeted information right into the hands of your best prospects. Plus, consumers like to read them, probably because they tend to be short and to the point. That's important, given how busy people are and how short their attention spans can be. (Think 30-second sound bites and Xbox games.)

Informational newsletters tend to work best for auto detailing professionals. A typical newsletter might contain checklists ("Six Ways to Make Your Car Really Shine"), information about detailing products ("The Three Products You Should Never Use on Leather"), facts about how the weather can damage a vehicle's finish, and so on. Even though it might seem like you're giving away secrets, you're actually subtly selling your own services. You simply add a tag line to the end of each story that touts your expertise. For example, on the weather story, you could end with a line that says something like, "Great Lakes Automotive Detailing can help your car weather a hard Michigan winter in prime condition. Call (555) 555-0000 for a no-obligation quote." If you run specials or sales or if you want to try offering a coupon for a service, you can promote this in the newsletter as well.

In keeping with the trend toward short, quick reads, limit your newsletter to just two pages, that is, a single 8.5-by-11-inch sheet printed on the front and back (or designed as a two-page .pdf file for an e-newsletter). This size works great because it's inexpensive to produce—you can do it yourself on a photocopier at Kinko's—and it can be mailed in a No. 10 business-size envelope. And don't think you have to mail a lot of newsletters frequently to make your point. Two issues a year timed with the seasons, like a "spring cleaning" issue and an autumn issue with winterizing tips, should do the trick.

Although you'll probably want to use your newsletter to prospect for new business, it also can be sent to your existing client base. It's a great way to remind customers that they need to call for a detailing appointment, while giving you the opportunity to upsell, or suggest additional services your clients might be interested in.

Writing and Producing the Newsletter

Unless you have some writing experience, getting the words right can be the hardest part of doing a newsletter. The best way to get your message across effectively is to start each story with the most important information, followed by details that support your main point.

If you're not comfortable writing anything more complex than a grocery list or you've forgotten more grammar than you remember, you probably should hire a freelance writer to pen the newsletter for you. You can find a freelancer through local professional advertising organizations, the chamber of commerce, university journalism programs, and even the Yellow Pages. Depending on the experience of the writer, you can expect to pay $150 to $300 for a two-page newsletter.

Free Publicity

The media are always looking for interesting stories to fill space on a page or on the air, and people are always interested in services that can help make their lives easier. (Just think of the popularity of cable networks like DIY.) Keep your name out in front of the public as much as you can by trying some of these less-conventional promotional strategies:

○ *Become an expert.* Promote yourself as a local expert on all things related to vehicle maintenance and restoration by sending regular bulletins about detailing to the local media. Example: You just took a paintless dent repair course and the weather forecast calls for a freak hailstorm. Don't be shy—fax over a one-page news release to alert the media about how to handle hail damage. Include your business name and phone number prominently, and you could find yourself on the evening news.

○ *Make a donation.* Donate a professional service—say, a full detailing—to your local public TV station for its annual auction. Or donate a tool (like a polisher) or a box of detailing products that can be auctioned. Anthony Orosco of Ultimate Reflections in San Antonio does this regularly and recently donated three full detailings, valued at $300 each, for an American Heart Association auction. "Every chance one gets to socialize and talk shop with potential clients gets your name out there even more, and then you will be known as an expert in your profession," he says.

○ *Support your community.* Donate materials or time to help a local environmental group or civic club. Your benevolence will resonate throughout the community.

○ *Take up a cause.* Actively supporting environmental protection can put you in the spotlight. But avoid controversial issues and politics. Whichever side you take, you'll alienate the people who support the other side.

You might find that designing the newsletter is somewhat easier than writing the stories. There are a number of affordable desktop publishing software packages that come with newsletter templates. You just type in the headlines, paste in the copy, and *voilà*—the program does the copy fitting and formatting. One program you can try is Microsoft Publisher, which is bundled in the Microsoft Office package.

If you'd rather detail cars than design newsletters, you can hire a graphic designer to create a template for you in a software program like Microsoft Publisher. Then you can reuse that template each time you produce another newsletter. You'll pay around $300 or so (or $30 to $60 per hour) for a two-pager. Check the Yellow Pages under "Graphic Designers" or contact an art school to find a designer.

> ### Bright Idea
> If you're going after commercial business, like dealerships, create a pocket folder media kit for business prospects. Items in the kit may include a letter thanking the client for his/her interest, a service brochure or flier, copies of any articles written about the business, and information about you and your qualifications.

You can make your newsletter design more exciting and interesting by adding artwork. If you're doing an e-newsletter, feel free to use photos of vehicles you've detailed. But avoid photographs if you're going to photocopy the newsletter—the reproduction quality will be terrible, and the newsletter won't look professional. Another option is clip art, which is very inexpensive and easy to use. An all-purpose clip art package includes auto art that you can use over and over. You can also use the clip art on other promotional materials you create, like fliers. A good clip art package to try is ClickArt 400,000 from Broderbund, which retails for $29.99. In addition, Microsoft Word comes with a small selection of clip art, and you can go online to select from a wider assortment of images.

Feature Articles

If you have a flair for writing, you should consider writing feature stories as a way to increase your business's visibility. Newspapers (both the dailies and community papers) are always happy to look at articles that touch on subjects their readers would be interested in. Stories popular with newspaper editors include informational articles and how-tos (how to apply wax, how to use a buffer). As with newsletters, you're not just giving away trade secrets by sharing your knowledge and insight with readers; you're positioning yourself as an authority in your field.

Prentice St. Clair, the San Diego detailer, has forged a whole new career for himself writing articles for publications like *Modern Car Care*. He's published more than 90 articles on a wide variety of detailing and automotive reconditioning topics and is a regular contributor to two of the industry's leading trade publications. So go ahead—you can do it, too. Write articles giving tips for applying wax properly. Share stories about home detailing disasters and tell how they can be fixed or averted. Or report on a fleet of vehicles you detailed for the local millionaire. The possibilities are endless. Feature articles for newspapers usually run 800 to 1,000 words depending on the publication.

Submitting Your Manuscript

A manuscript can be submitted in one of three ways: by typing it on 8.5-by-11-inch white bond paper with one-inch margins on all sides, saving in text format on CD or floppy disk, or e-mailing it (attach the file *and* paste the text into the e-mail in case the editor doesn't open attachments). The manuscript should be accompanied by a brief pitch letter that briefly tells what the article is about and why it would appeal to the readers of the publication. Always call the publication to find out the name of the editor so your letter can be addressed properly (just think how you feel receiving "Dear Occupant" mail), and be sure to provide contact information so the editor can reach you later. Call the editor a few days after you send the article to find out whether it was appropriate for his/her audience and what you can do in the future to increase your chances of being published.

Networking

As you know from Chapter 9, there are only a few organizations nationwide that cater to the needs of detailing professionals. When you find them, join them, then participate in their meetings and activities, because networking is a very good way to gain exposure for your venture and possibly drum up new business.

You'll also benefit from memberships in business organizations like your local chamber of commerce and the Rotary Club. Besides meeting the owners of both small and large businesses in your community—people who may themselves need a detailer in the future—you can exchange ideas for doing business better and possibly barter services (like trading a full-service detail for printing). The cost to join such organizations is usually nominal and is deductible as a business expense.

Tip...

Smart Tip

When attending networking events sponsored by professional business organizations, circulate and meet as many people as possible since everyone is a potential trade/exchange/bartering partner. Just be sure to make notations on the backs of any business cards you receive so you'll remember later why the person might be a valuable contact in the future.

Public Speaking Engagements

Americans love their cars, so what better place to talk about your detailing expertise than at car clinics, car meets, and cruises? While some events might charge you a nominal fee to set up a booth, others may be free—and still others may actually pay *you* to be on hand.

The next time you hear about an event where lots of car lovers will congregate, find out what you can do to get a spot on the fairway, on the route, or on the panel. Then come prepared to talk about detailing in general and to answer specific questions from your adoring public. And be sure to slip in references to your own business whenever possible, as in "That's a great question, sir. At Great Lakes Automotive Detailing, we use a chamois to apply products because it's nonabrasive and lint-free."

Also, never underestimate the power of trade shows—even home and garden shows—for drumming up new business. "I've done the Annapolis Boat Show, where 90,000 people walked past my booth," says Mike Myers of Gem Auto Appearance Center in Waldorf, Maryland. "Whenever I'd give out a card, I'd say, 'Take two, take more, because if you have your car or boat done, others will want theirs done, too.' One job will sell the next two jobs."

One last tip for making an impression at an industry or consumer event: Take along a supply of advertising specialty items, like pens imprinted with your business name and address, to give away to the people you meet. They're surprisingly inexpensive, and they tend to find their way into people's pockets or desk drawers, where they serve as a reminder that you're ready and willing to detail the heck out of their prized vehicles. A quick search of the internet showed that one company is offering 500 Bic Clic pens personalized with your company name for about $297, whereas another sells 1,000 neon stick-up calendars for $270, which is just 27 cents each.

Calendars are another good giveaway item. Small pocket-sized calendars imprinted with your company name and address are a good choice because people tend to carry them around with them and pull them out for all to see. To find a supplier for giveaway items, check the "Advertising Specialties" listing in the phone book.

Bright Idea

A sure-fire way to get good publicity—and new business—is by sharing your detailing know-how in do-it-yourself detail workshops. Gary Kouba of Perfect Auto Finish in Roseville, Illinois, does this regularly and reports he gets a lot of business from attendees who realize detailing is a lot of work and best left to the pros.

Financial Fit
and Finish

Now that you've worked your way through
this owner's manual and figured out all the standard equipment you need to start detailing for a living, it's time for a final
tune-up that will enable you to fuel up your finances so you can
embark on the ride of your life.

▲

As you know, money is the engine that makes every business run. But it's the management of that money that makes the business last. It's not enough to be the best detailer in the city of (fill in the blank). You also have to know how much money is going out so you know how much you have to bring in. You have to be able to project sales and adjust staffing accordingly. You have to contain costs so you can put aside enough to stay afloat when business is slow during the winter or when inclement weather shuts you down. And above all, you need to have enough cash left over after expenses to make the installment payments on life's many obligations.

Fortunately, you don't have to be a financial genius or hold a business degree to do all this. With the help of an accounting software package, a good accountant, and tried-and-true accounting methods, you can keep your business on the road to profitability. But in addition to persistence, it will take serious financial backing or sufficient personal resources if you're planning a site-based operation as well as a keen interest in the state of your finances, whether you're building-bound or mobile. It also will take a certain amount of fortitude, because the start-up period of any business is labor-intensive and difficult, and the early years can be very lean.

In this chapter, we present all the financial liabilities you'll encounter on the way to earning a living from your detailing business. Then it will be up to you to generate the income to offset those expenses and make a profit. So, ladies and gentlemen, start your engines, and let's get cranking.

Looks Good

If you're leasing your building, chances are exterior work like snow removal and grass cutting will be included in your monthly lease payment. But if you bought it, you're responsible for all the upkeep. While maintenance cuts into detailing time, it's a crucial part of operations because the appearance of your building and property are a reflection on the work you do. Interior upkeep, including emptying trash, sweeping and washing floors, and cleaning the bathroom should be the responsibility of every employee, although it probably will be necessary to assign someone to do each job so it actually gets done. Laundry should be everyone's responsibility, since an average-size shop probably will have to do a couple of loads of laundry daily to keep up with usage. In addition to loading up the machines, everyone should pitch in to fluff and fold.

Overall cleanliness is really important, especially in the restroom, according to Tom Schurmann, former owner of Masterfinish in Lakewood, Colorado. "I had people comment on how rare it is to go into an auto shop with a clean bathroom," he says. "If I won't go into the bathroom myself, I wouldn't expect someone else to, so our bathrooms were always spotless."

Operating Income and Expenses

This snapshot of your prospective business may look positively terrifying when you start filling in the numbers. Every month, you will have more essential expenses than lug nuts on a convoy of 18-wheelers, and you may have to steel yourself against the shock it causes to your system. But it's critical to keep track of debits and credits so you always know where you stand.

Although you can have your accountant create an operating income/expenses (I&E) statement for you, you might want to try doing it yourself using the simple worksheet on page 142, or using an accounting package like QuickBooks. In the meantime, we've given you samples on pages 140 and 141 that show the operating income and expenses for two hypothetical detailing businesses. The first business, Details on Wheels, is a mobile business whose owner flies solo, while Executive Auto Restoration & Detail is a fixed-location business that supports two part-time employees in addition to the owner. We've estimated monthly costs for each to give you an idea how much a new business might incur. Among these costs are the following.

Mortgage/Rent

If you're operating out of a facility, this will be one of your largest monthly expenditures. As with any other mortgage, your payments are due on the same day each month, and unless your mortgage is adjustable, the amount will always be the same. So all you have to do is plug this number into your I&E.

Phone

Ever since the telecommunications industry was deregulated years ago, phone rates have gone wild as telephone companies duke it out for dominance. So you'll need to check with your local phone company to determine which number to plug into your I&E. Charges can vary widely, but it's reasonable to estimate a cost of $25 per line. Voice mail is about $6 to $20 per month, call waiting is approximately $5 per month, and caller ID is about $7.50 for number identification and $2 extra for name display. Caller ID is especially useful if you're using your home phone as your business line.

If you're doing business in a small to midsized market, you probably can start out with a single phone line in addition to your personal phone line. If you call a major metropolitan area home, it

Beware!
To avoid problems if you're ever audited, keep a log of business calls, then compare it against your phone bill every month. The IRS usually requires written records for any expenses you deduct, and it will be much easier to figure which calls are legitimate business expenses if you have a log to refer back to.

Operating Income/Expenses

Here are sample operating income/expense statements for two hypothetical detailing companies that reflect typical operating costs for this industry. Details on Wheels is a one-person sole proprietorship while Executive Auto Restoration & Detail is a C corporation with one full-time employee (the owner), two part-time technicians, and a 3,000-square-foot detailing shop in a large metropolitan area. Use the worksheet provided on page 142 to project your own income and expenses.

Details on Wheels

Projected monthly income	*$4,500*
Projected monthly expenses	
Mortgage/rent	0
Phone (office and cell)	$90
Utilities (water only)	$50
Postage	$10
Licenses	$20
Owner's salary	$2,500
Employee wages	0
Benefits/taxes	0
Advertising/promotion	$90
Legal services	$20
Accounting services	$50
Merchant account	$30
Supplies	$50
Insurance	$125
Transportation/maintenance	$100
Subscriptions/dues	$150
Loan repayment	$360
Online services	$40
Miscellaneous	$368
TOTAL EXPENSES	*$4,053*
Projected Income/Expense Total	*$447*

Executive Auto Restoration & Detail

Projected monthly income   *$11,000*

Projected monthly expenses

Mortgage/rent	$1,200
Phone (office and cell)	$90
Utilities (water only)	$100
Postage	$25
Licenses	$20
Owner's salary	$3,750
Employee wages	$1,600
Benefits/taxes	$350
Advertising/promotion	$550
Legal services	$75
Accounting services	$50
Merchant account	$30
Supplies	$100
Insurance	$225
Transportation/maintenance	$50
Subscriptions/dues	$50
Loan repayment	$560
Online services	$40
Miscellaneous	$887

TOTAL EXPENSES   *$9,752*

Projected Income/Expense Total   *$1,248*

Operating Income/Expenses Worksheet

Projected monthly income $_____

Projected monthly expenses

Mortgage/rent	$_____
Phone (office and cell)	$_____
Utilities	$_____
Postage	$_____
Licenses	$_____
Owner's salary	$_____
Employee wages	$_____
Benefits/taxes	$_____
Advertising/promotion	$_____
Legal services	$_____
Accounting services	$_____
Merchant account	$_____
Supplies	$_____
Insurance	$_____
Transportation/maintenance	$_____
Subscriptions/dues	$_____
Loan repayment	$_____
Online services	$_____
Miscellaneous	$_____

TOTAL EXPENSES $_____

Projected Income/Expense Total $_____

might be a good idea to have at least two business lines. The second line also could be used for your fax machine and dial-up internet service, but be sure to have voice mail on that line so callers won't ever get a busy signal. If you're mobile and handling the administrative duties out of a corner of your living room, you still should consider having a second business line. You don't want your two-year-old to win the race to pick up the family phone. Install that second line in a place where only you will answer it.

Your cellular phone bill is also a legitimate business expense that can go on your I&E as long as it's used strictly for business. Basic packages start as low as $9.95 and go up to as much as $69.95 for plans with multiple phones and a gazillion airtime minutes.

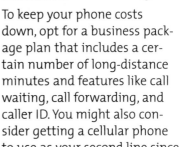

Dollar Stretcher

To keep your phone costs down, opt for a business package plan that includes a certain number of long-distance minutes and features like call waiting, call forwarding, and caller ID. You might also consider getting a cellular phone to use as your second line since rates are now so affordable.

Utilities

As mentioned in Chapter 7, site-based detailing shops need special plumbing to meet EPA regulations, plus they run a lot of powerful electrical equipment like generators, some of which may draw extra current. As a result, your utility bills may be high. To come up with a reliable estimate, check with your local city government offices to find out which utilities provide local services, then call their customer service departments and ask the representative to help you estimate your monthly bills. Be sure to mention what kind of work you do when you call (since you'll need more water than, say, a bookstore) as well as the square footage of your facility, so you'll get the most accurate estimates.

Postage

As mentioned in Chapter 10, you may want to do a mass mailing a few times a year to entice new prospects to use your services. First-class postage is an option, but you might be able to qualify for a reduced bulk rate. Just keep in mind that bulk mail is often perceived as junk mail, and the recipient may toss your carefully crafted advertising piece without even opening it. Also, if you anticipate having any monthly shipping charges (like for shipping retail products to customers), estimate and include those, too.

Licenses

It's quite likely you'll only need one type of license to open your doors: a business license that's renewable annually. You get it from the licensing department of the city in which you're based, and the cost varies by city. We're using $20 on our sample I&E just for simplicity's sake.

▲

In addition, you'll need to buy renewable transport tags if you will be picking up and delivering dealership or customer vehicles. They're available from your state's department of motor vehicles or secretary of state, and although the cost can vary by state, you can expect to pay around $125 per tag.

Owner's Salary

Naturally, the salary you take from the business has to be figured in on the I&E to get a clear picture of the business's monthly expenses. Some detailers have the luxury of relying on a spouse's salary and benefits so most of the profits from the detailing business can be plowed back into the business to make it grow faster, but chances are you'll be taking a draw. Think carefully before you fill in this number on your I&E. Although you'll want to cover everyday expenses, you may find that making a few financial sacrifices now could benefit the business tremendously later.

However, Anthony Orosco of Ultimate Reflections in San Antonio recommends setting up a separate payroll account and paying yourself a regular salary even if the amount is irregular. "When you want to purchase something like a house or a car, you'll need to show a regular income," he says. "You may still have to show your tax returns for major purchases, but it looks better if you can show consistency in paying yourself."

Employee Wages

Wages will take a big bite out of your operating budget—possibly 30 to 40 percent of the cost of every vehicle you detail. You can keep your expenses down by keeping wages down, but you'll have unhappy employees who will think nothing of jumping ship as soon as a better offer comes along.

All the entrepreneurs interviewed for this book pay their employees a few dollars over minimum wage, and all report having very good retention rates. The wage range was from $6.50 to $10 an hour. Prentice St. Clair of Detail in Progress in San Diego also pays a bonus on top of the hourly wage as a way to keep employees motivated.

Tom Schurmann, former owner of Masterfinish in Lakewood, Colorado, preferred paying on a system known as piece work. "I paid my technicians 33 percent of the gross invoice with the understanding that the work had to be done right the first time," Schurmann says. "All work was quality-checked before the vehicle left the shop, and if anything had to be redone, it was done for free. That made employees pay more attention to the job they were doing."

For the sake of our hypothetical I&E operating expenses statement calculations, we've used the following wages:

Owner: $45,000 per year (salaried)

Technician: $7.75/an hour

Benefits/Taxes

Benefits are another expense that will cut deeply into your monthly income. For this reason, detailers often don't offer benefits other than perhaps a one-week paid vacation and the occasional sick day. Although benefits do make people happy, it's not always necessary to offer them. Tom Schurmann found that even when he offered to pay half the cost of health insurance, his employees didn't want a penny deducted from their checks. One of the reasons was because his technicians already had spouses with full-time jobs and full benefits. So he opted instead to pay a little more than the average for the piecework they did, and everyone seemed happy.

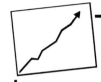

Stat Fact
The U.S. Department of Labor reports that in 2002 benefits comprised 27.9 percent of total employee compensation. However, detailers are nowhere near that league—you're more likely to pay 8 to 10 percent in benefits costs, if you offer any at all. To figure that cost into your I&E, multiply the figure on the employee wages line by .08.

Figuring out the tax portion of the amount on the benefits/tax line is a little trickier. As we discussed in Chapter 8, there's a whole slew of taxes you'll have to pay on employees' wages, including the FICA tax, Federal Unemployment Tax and state unemployment tax, and workers' compensation insurance. Since you don't have previous records to compare to, you should estimate high so you're not caught short. Your accountant can help you make a reasonable guess.

Once you've calculated both the benefits and the tax figures, add them together, divide by 12 and enter that figure on the benefits/tax line.

Advertising/Promotion

You'll want to estimate the cost of producing fliers, direct-mail pieces, newspaper advertising, and any other business awareness efforts you may decide to do. Yellow Pages advertising costs would also go here. Rather than trying to figure out to the penny how much you'll spend and painstakingly slot it into the appropriate month where it will be spent, get estimates on all the costs, add them up, divide by 12, and plop that figure in here.

Legal Services

These fees can be a little difficult to estimate because you may not have regular monthly expenses. As mentioned in Chapter 5, some attorneys work on retainers, in which case you would include the whole amount of that cost on your start-up expenses worksheet. If you use an attorney who works on a project basis, just guesstimate the number of hours you'll need his/her services, multiply that by the hourly rate, and

▲

include one-twelfth of that amount on your I&E. If you're going with a package of basic start-up services and don't anticipate using the attorney much after that, include the entire amount on your start-up worksheet and nothing on your I&E. You can always add a dollar figure into the "Miscellaneous" category later to cover any unexpected legal fees.

Accounting Services

While basic bookkeeping is pretty easy when you use QuickBooks or Peachtree, you should use an accountant for the more complex accounting chores (including business taxes). Accountants are generally compensated on an hourly basis, so find out his/her rate, multiply that by a reasonable number of hours (say, ten a month), and use that figure on your I&E.

Merchant Account

Because detailing services tend to be pricey, it's unlikely that your clients will pay you with cold, hard cash (especially if you're detailing in the great outdoors). You can certainly accept checks or the occasional greenbacks, but you should also seriously consider establishing a merchant account that will allow you to accept credit and debit cards.

A merchant account is basically a clearinghouse for electronic payments. After swiping a credit or debit card through a point-of-sale (POS) terminal (discussed in detail in Chapter 6), you'll get an authorization code that tells you the customer's credit is good. The funds from that purchase eventually will find their way into your account, less a discount rate—which is a fixed percentage of anywhere from 1.5 to 4 percent per transaction—deducted from the purchase by the merchant account provider. There are other fees associated with merchant account maintenance, which typically include a statement fee of about $10 a month and a small fee for each transaction processed (usually around 20 cents). You also may have to pay a programming fee to get the whole shebang established, a monthly minimum fee, a "gateway" fee (for secure payments), a chargeback processing fee, etc. Since this is one industry that is pretty darned creative when it comes to fees, it pays to shop around for the best rates. To get you started, we've provided contact information in the Appendix for several merchant account providers. In the meantime, we've optimistically marked down a merchant account fee of $30 per month on the sample I&E statements on pages 140 and 141.

> ## Smart Tip
> *Tip...*
>
> Before you can offer customers the convenience of paying with a major credit card, you must establish a merchant account through a bank or an independent sales organization (an organization that represents a bank or processor), after which you can buy a credit card imprinting device.

Incidentally, if you're mobile, you'll have to go wireless to have a merchant account, which means you'll have your choice of really cool processing options and equipment. Wireless processing can now be done by cell phone or laptop, with a system known as AirPay Solution, with a two-way pager and a magnetic card reader, or with a wireless portable POS swipe terminal. One company that can hook you up with all these equipment and processing services is MerchantSeek, which can be found on the Internet at www.merchantseek.com/mcommerce.htm.

Supplies

Since you're going to need a lot of different supplies for the business, you might want to separate the two main types of supplies: On one hand, you'll need assorted polishes, buffer pads, clay bars, towels, and all the other stuff discussed in Chapter 6; on the other, you'll need pens, legal pads, computer paper, and other supplies to run the business. For the expenses you don't incur every month, like business printing, just use the figure you got when you priced your business cards and divide it by 12 so you can come up with a monthly estimate that can be added to this amount.

Cash, Check, or Charge?

Since detailing is a big-ticket purchase, you'll have to offer your customers the option of using credit cards. So an important expense you'll incur monthly will be point-of-sale processing costs for accepting Visa, MasterCard, and other credit cards, as well as debit cards. The rates vary among the many merchant account services around. One company we found had a $10 per month statement fee, a 20-cents-per-transaction fee, and a discount of 1.5 percent (meaning you pay the merchant account company 1.5 percent of each transaction). Another company included free web hosting, a free business checking account, and other valuable services as part of its merchant account service. You'll want to shop around carefully for the best deal.

If you're planning to accept personal checks, a check verification service is also a good idea because it can reduce your risk of accepting a bad check. The cost is similar to that of a merchant account, and usually includes a discount fee on all checks you accept (rarely lower than 1.79 percent, according to MerchantSeek.com), a per-item transaction fee of 15 to 25 cents, and possibly a monthly minimum fee, a statement fee, and an application fee. But what you get is the best possible verification that every check you accept is good. Again, it pays to shop around for the best rates.

Insurance

Using the worksheet on page 58, tally up the amount of commercial garagekeeper's liability insurance you plan to carry, and divide that figure by 12 to come up with a number for this line. By the way, if you're using a personal vehicle like a van or SUV for your business that also doubles in off-hours as transportation for the family, you'll have to keep careful records about the percentage of time the vehicle is used strictly for business. Be sure to deduct those detours to pick up the kids from school during business hours or trips through the drive-thru window at McDonald's for dinner on your way home. The easiest way to keep track of these numbers is by keeping a simple mileage log. Office supply stores sell mileage logbooks that are small enough to stash in your glove compartment or in a pocket of your visor. Make sure you jot down business mileage every time you get behind the wheel, or your records won't be acceptable to the IRS.

Beware!

If your family vehicle doubles as your business transportation, be sure to keep careful records on the number of miles you drive for business. The IRS will only let you deduct the percentage of the insurance costs, the loan payment, maintenance, gasoline, etc., that pertains to the business.

Transportation/Maintenance

If you're mobile, keeping your truck or other vehicle in good working order is paramount since you'll be out of business if it's not reliable and ready to go when you are. Tally up the cost of regular tune-ups, then add in an amount to cover regular maintenance, like oil changes and spark plug replacement. Also add in the estimated cost of gasoline, windshield wiper fluid, and any travel-related costs, as well as vehicle payments if appropriate. We've estimated $100 per month for a mobile business and $50 a month for a site-based detailer.

Subscriptions/Dues

As discussed in Chapter 9, reading magazines and trade publications is a good way to stay current on issues of importance to detailers, so you'll probably want to subscribe to a number of different detailing and carwash publications. And don't forget to stock up the waiting area with car magazines as well as general interest publications like *People, Better Homes and Gardens*, and *Newsweek*. It would probably also be a good idea to put a few children's books out for the kiddies. Put them all in an attractive magazine stand in your waiting room, then add their cost (because this is a legitimate business expense) to your operating statement.

Among the types of membership dues you'll want to include here are the costs to join industry-related organizations and local business organizations like the chamber of commerce. Refer back to Chapter 9 for a list of the major organizations that have ties to the detailing industry.

Loan Repayment

Whether you borrowed money for a down payment on your building, for equipment, or for a vehicle loan, that figure has to go on your monthly expense report. This is also where you'd include any loans from family, friends, and investors (discussed later in the financing section).

Online Services

The average rate for dial-up services is $14.95 to $19.95 a month, although you can find bargain rates that are lower. A DSL or high-speed cable connection can cost $50 a month, while web hosting charges for 1,000MB of space can be as low as $9.95 per month.

Miscellaneous Expenses

This is a catch-all category for items like coffee for the waiting room, trash bags for collecting loose items left in a customer's vehicle, and cleaning supplies for the restroom. Adding in 10 percent of bottom-line total is usually sufficient to cover these miscellaneous expenses.

Receivables

Everything we've just talked about is the red ink on your balance sheet. Your receivables are what the black ink is made of. To help you get to that happy point when the black beats red (kind of like in rock-paper-scissors), use the accounting software of your choice so you'll always have a running total of where the business stands.

Forecasting Receivables

Here's a simple way to estimate how much money you'll need to earn to stay solvent and make a profit. Let's use Executive Auto Restoration & Detail as an example of how to do this rudimentary estimate. If the three-bay detailing shop's total expenses (including wages) for the month are $8,000, and the owner, Mark Lindsay, charges $125 for a full detailing, he and his staff will have to give 64 vehicles the works each month just to break even. Of course, Mark has additional training in paintless dent repair and window repair, and doing just 15 of these special services at $150 each per month would result automatically in a profit of $2,250, less the cost of supplies and labor. That just goes to show you that whereas regular detailing services will be the mainstay of your business, restoration services can quickly add extra bucks to your bottom line.

Now it's your turn. Figure out the dollar amount of the services you'll need to render, then keep that in mind as we discuss the process of collecting money for your hard work.

Collecting the Cash

Most detailers work on a cash or credit basis with payment due when the services are rendered. For this reason, you'll need to be able to generate a bill of sale or receipt when customers are ready to pay up. Programs like QuickBooks have a receipt template you can fill out to create a computer-generated bill when cashing out clients. If you're mobile, you should generate this receipt before you head out to a job or carry a small receipt book (available at any office supply store) that can be filled out when the customer pays.

If you work for dealerships or you have big-ticket customers like Waldorf, Maryland-based Gem Auto Appearance Center owner Mike Myers' boat customers, you may have to invoice them instead. We've included an invoice on page 151, plus you can find a template you can use in MS Excel. Be sure to bill regularly—monthly or biweekly—to make sure your cash flow is steady and so clients remember they had the service.

Bookkeeping Solutions

We've already alluded to accounting and business software several times in this chapter as affordable and user-friendly for many of your financial needs. Even if your last math class was in 12th grade, you can easily get the hang of the inner workings of one of these packages. One of the best reasons to rely on one of these programs for financial assistance is that it'll help you avoid inadvertent math errors that can throw your calculations off.

The most popular choice of the detailers we interviewed was QuickBooks by Intuit. The Pro version for Windows retails for $299.95, and besides having an invoice template, it helps you track receivables, write checks, pay bills, and more. It also interfaces with Microsoft Word, Excel, and other software. Another plus, data from QuickBooks can be imported directly into income tax preparation packages like Turbo Tax. Even if you'd rather leave taxing matters to your accountant, you'll probably find that QuickBooks will interface with his or her tax software as well. You can find QuickBooks at office supply and computer stores.

Another popular accounting package you might like to try is Peachtree Accounting. It retails for $199.95 and is available from computer stores and directly from Peachtree (www.peachtree.com).

INVOICE

Sold to: Mr. Greg Jakub
             5555 Allard
             Grosse Pointe Woods, Michigan 48236

Description of services:

Interior Detailing

Vacuuming, plastic and vinyl/leather cleaning, conditioning	$29.95
Deodorizing	$25.00

Exterior Detailing
Hand wash and dry, buff and wax	$39.95
Engine cleaning	$49.95
Tires dressed	$15.00

TOTAL   *$159.85*

Thank you!

Daniel Wayne
Owner
Great Lakes Automotive Detailing

5555 Jefferson Ave. · St. Clair Shores, Michigan 48051 · (555) 555-0000
www.greatlakesdetailing.com · info@greatlakesdetailing.com

▲

The Cash Kings

Now that you have a pretty good picture of what it will cost to run your detailing business every month, you may also be painfully aware that you'll need some financial assistance to make your dream a reality, especially if you're going the facility route. The most logical source of funding is your friendly local bank, but you may find it's difficult to get the big boys to play ball with you. That's because the megarich banks are usually more interested in funding large companies that need large amounts of capital, because that's how they make big money. They're also sometimes reluctant to deal with one-person and start-up companies simply because such ventures don't have a lengthy track record of success.

To navigate your way around this problem, you'll have to shop around to find a bank that will welcome the opportunity to work with you. "Small-business owners usually do better by selecting a bank with a community banking philosophy," says Robert Sisson, vice president and commercial business manager of Citizens Bank in Sturgis, Michigan, and author of *Show Me the Money*. "These are the banks that support their communities and function almost as much like a consultant as a bank."

So bypass the big regional banks, and check out the smaller financial institutions instead, because they are more willing to accommodate small-business customers, according to Wendy Thomas, senior business consultant at the Michigan Small Business Development Center at the One Stop Capital Shop in Detroit. "Small banks are simply more willing to deal with small-business concerns and are more sensitive to issues like the need for longer accounts-receivable periods," Thomas says.

Alternatively, you could approach your local credit union for financing. Credit unions are nonprofit, cooperative financial institutions owned and run by their members and are

---

The Five C's

All banks use certain factors to determine a business's creditworthiness. These criteria include:

- ○ *Collateral:* assets to secure the loan,
- ○ *Capital:* owner's equity,
- ○ *Conditions:* anything that affects the financial climate,
- ○ *Character:* personal credit history, and
- ○ *Cash flow:* ability to support debts, expenses.

generally more generous with rates, terms, and conditions. They may be more willing to assist you, but only if you're a member. But since there's a credit union for practically every organized group (including teachers, churches, military branches, and so on), it's likely you can find one in your area you can join.

And by the way, when you're at the bank or credit union, open a business checking account. You absolutely must keep your personal and business finances separate, even if you're a one-person business with a modest income.

> **Tip...**
>
> ## Smart Tip
>
> Banks use three measures to determine your business's ability to make a profit: the gross profit margin, the operating profit margin, and the net profit margin. The decision to lend is made based on this information because it's the best indication of whether you're a good financial risk.

Help from Your Favorite Uncle

The U.S. government is actually pretty small-business-friendly. For one, the SBA is devoted to small-business issues and resources. And, although the government defines a small business as any enterprise with fewer than 500 employees, it will be just as willing to help your one-person company as it would be to assist a whole chain of detailing superstores.

One way the SBA can be of particular assistance to you if you're planning to hit up a bank for financing is with its free counseling and training seminars on topics like business plan and marketing plan development. The SBA can provide you with tips and strategies you can use to make yourself and your fledgling company look more attractive to a bank. The SBA also offers a number of loan programs, if you want to bypass the banks completely, as well as counseling and training. For more information, check the SBA's web site at www.sba.gov or call the answer desk at (800) 8-ASK-SBA.

Do-It-Yourself Financing

If you've always been a saver or you're starting a mobile business (which generally has much lower start-up costs than a site-based business), you may not need the assistance of the big lenders to get the appropriate start-up stake. Sometimes personal savings are enough to pay for the basics, especially when supplemented with a small unsecured personal loan from a bank or credit union. Unsecured loans are much easier to obtain than business loans, assuming you have good credit and a record of paying your debts on time. If you decide to go this route, consider every source of personal capital you may have, including savings accounts and certificates of deposit; income tax refunds; stocks and bonds; savings bonds; real estate, vehicles, and personal assets like jewelry (all of which can be sold to raise cash); and retirement funds like pension plans, IRAs, 401(k) plans, SEPs, and Keoghs. A lot of people prefer not to touch retirement plan funds because there's a penalty for cashing out before age 59½. But if your business is successful, you can easily recoup those penalties, so raiding the pension funds may be a viable option.

If your personal savings just amount to a nest egg, you might consider using a home equity line of credit loan to cover initial costs—assuming your bank is willing to give you one for a business start-up. Just be very aware that if the unthinkable happens and your business doesn't succeed, your home is the collateral and would be sold by the bank to recoup its money. If you don't have a high tolerance for stress, another source of financing might be more advisable.

Personal credit cards are yet another common source of start-up cash, although you have to make sure you watch your expenses closely. You don't want to skimp on equipment and tools, but when you're using plastic, it's always tempting to buy stuff with all the bells and whistles when just the basics will do. Get the best you afford without spending big bucks so you don't start your business encumbered with a huge debt.

If all else fails, you could borrow money from friends and family, but of course that can be a sticky situation. Make sure to handle the transaction in a professional, businesslike way. Always sign a promissory note that details repayment terms and offers an equitable interest rate, then faithfully make payments on the loan just like you'd make payments on your car or mortgage. This is critical if you go for this kind of unconventional financing because you don't want to break up your family or lose a lifelong friend over a broken promise of repayment or a misunderstanding about how it will be handled.

> **Bright Idea**
> To determine whether your local bank is small-business-friendly, review its annual reports for information about its financial focus and business outlook, the type of loans it makes to small companies, and the types of businesses it services, all of which are clues about the bank's commitment to the community.

The Fast Lane
to Success

This is it—the final lap before you take the wheel of your own detailing business. It's our sincerest hope that the information you have read in this start–up manual will put you on the road to success and prosperity in your new profession. But even as we wish you well in your new venture, we would be remiss if we didn't point out one very sobering fact:

▲

There is the distinct possibility that even with a solid foundation, sufficient funding, and boundless enthusiasm, your business may not succeed.

Business failure tends to occur among smaller firms because they're often underfunded, poorly managed, or unprepared for economic downturns. But just remember: Henry Ford attempted and failed to start an automobile company several times before he succeeded with the Ford Motor Company.

So let's take a closer look at some reasons for business failure so you can figure out how to avoid being another unfavorable statistic.

> **Tip...**
>
> ## Smart Tip
>
> If you get into a cash–flow crunch, draft a plan to repay your creditors rather than just ignoring them until you have enough money to cover your debts. Most creditors will be willing to work with you because they stand more of a chance of getting their money back if you remain open than if you close.

Why Businesses Fail

Probably the number–one reason for business failure is inadequate cash reserves. Obviously, it will take a while to establish your business and build a reputation, so you may find you don't have a lot of customers in the early days. Make sure you have a sufficient nest egg to keep the business running and your personal expenses paid. Depending on your comfort level, you may want to have a six–month cushion or maybe even enough funds for a year. These funds can come from personal savings, or they can be part of the start–up stake you get from a bank. No matter where it comes from, just make sure the money is readily available when you need it, even if you have to stash it in a low–interest savings account.

The SBA says that outside market conditions, including new competition or unexpected increases in the cost of doing business, also can contribute to business failure, as can tax problems, poor planning, and mismanagement. The SBA Online Women's Business Center adds these additional reasons for business failure:

- Overgeneralizing and trying to be everything for everyone, which can diminish quality
- Failure to define and understand your market, your customers, and your customers' buying habits
- Failure to price your products or services correctly
- Failure to anticipate cash flow adequately
- Failure to anticipate or react to competition, technology, or other changes in the marketplace
- Believing you can do everything yourself

Your Plan of Action

So how can you avoid these pitfalls and have the best chance at success in your new venture? Start by hiring professionals, like attorneys and accountants, to assist with business management chores. Those are what they do best, and hiring them frees you up to do what you do best. We know it can be pretty hard to part with the cash to pay their fees in the early days of a new business, but it's truly worth it in the long run.

Whenever possible, you also should learn as much as possible about business management techniques. Take a few courses at your local community college or university, or even through an adult education program. Just knowing the basics of finance, accounting, and marketing really can help you make better decisions that will keep you in business.

And finally, have a positive outlook. That might sound trite, but the fact is, entrepreneurs who are optimistic and have some chutzpah are often the most successful. Think of Donald Trump, who earned and lost a fortune, then earned it again; Ray Kroc, who took a humble hamburger and parlayed it into a fast–food empire; or Bill Gates, a self–professed nerd who founded an empire.

Is there anything these entrepreneurs–turned–billionaires would have done differently on their march to the top? Without a doubt. The same goes for detailers who have built successful careers out of nothing more than suds and solvents.

Anthony Orosco of Ultimate Reflections in San Antonio admits he should have shopped around for capital before starting his mobile business. "[Lack of capital] is the number–one reason why most detailers either fail or struggle," he says. "In the lean times, when work is slow or when you're [building] a client base, and you run out of money, it places a lot of pressure on the business, your marriage, and other personal and business relationships."

Gary Kouba of Perfect Auto Finish in Roselle, Illinois, wishes he had started his detailing career sooner. "I had been detailing cars since I was a kid, but I spent 20 years doing something else before I started a detailing business. But the passion for cars was always there," he says.

Waldorf, Maryland–based Mike Myers of Gem Auto Appearance Center (who started as a mobile detailer) wonders whether it might have been a better idea to stick with mobile detailing. "I probably was a much nicer guy [when I started out]," he says with a laugh. "Now I have two mortgages, a family, and a work family of six employees. I really enjoy detailing, but I don't do it much anymore. It always gave me a real sense of accomplishment—plus, no one could make a car look any better than I could."

Karen Duncan of Union Park Appearance Care Center in Wilmington, Delaware, would have instituted drug screening and driving record checks when she was in business for herself. "People present themselves well in an interview, then show their true colors after you've hired them. Checking these things would have cut out some mistakes," she says.

Dave Echnoz of 14/69 Carwash Supercenter in Fort Wayne, Indiana, encountered a lot of people who thought detailing was a humble profession not worthy of notice, and admits he shouldn't have let it bother him. "People used to shun me when they found out I managed a carwash and detail shop, and they still do, but of course I couldn't care less now," he says. "Even my own father didn't understand why I wanted to do this and used to try to get me to go to college. But when I built my second house—something he never had—he said to me, 'Dave, you've made it.' That was a great moment."

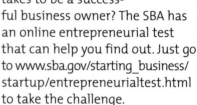

Fun Fact

Do you have what it takes to be a successful business owner? The SBA has an online entrepreneurial test that can help you find out. Just go to www.sba.gov/starting_business/startup/entrepreneurialtest.html to take the challenge.

Bay Watch

Even though the detailers interviewed for this book all believed there were things they could have done better at the genesis of their careers, not one had any real regrets. Rather, they worked hard and relied on their own natural enthusiasm, creative thinking, and determination to get them through the lean years. As a result, they managed to beat the odds against small–business ownership and build careers that have been rewarding in both personal and financial terms.

They've also accumulated a trunkload of experience on the trials and tribulations of what it takes to be a professional detailer. For example, there was the time that Mike Myers and two of his employees made the 90–minute trip to Baltimore's Inner Harbor to detail a boat. Upon arrival, they discovered no one had loaded the "laundry" (the buffing pads and towels they needed). So while his crew prepped the boat, Myers went shopping and ended up buying "nice towels like you'd use at home," as he puts it, so they could get the job done. "Now we have a laminated checklist on the dashboard of our mobile unit that shows everything we need, and it's the driver's responsibility to go over it before leaving," Myers says.

Tony Orosco and his former partner, John Hernandez, learned the importance of pricing services properly when they did their first boat detailing. Because they had no idea what was involved, they seriously underbid the job; then, when they got to the marina, they discovered the boat was not dry–docked. They ended up cleaning and polishing the hull from a tiny rowboat. In addition to getting seriously sunburned, they had to go back a second day to finish the job—all for $125. "That was our first and last boat detail in the water," Orosco says.

San Diego–based Prentice St. Clair discovered that an incredible piece of business can come from just about anywhere. One day when he was detailing cars in an office park, he was approached by the personal assistant of a multibillionaire who needed a detailer. He ended up detailing in the man's 60–car subterranean garage, which, among other things, held one of every Jaguar ever built.

Since detailing tends to be a man's world, it's not uncommon to run into chauvinistic attitudes, as Karen Duncan of Union Park Appearance Care Center in Wilmington, Delaware, found out. When she first started in the industry, men didn't take her seriously. "I can talk about cars like the best of them, but they treated me like I was just a receptionist and would ask to speak to a man about their vehicle," she says. "That faded over the years as I developed relationships with customers, and now people even ask me to go with them when they're ready to buy a car. I don't charge them—I just like to do it."

Gary Kouba proved that persistence is key to finding new work. He once walked out of Walgreens and saw a red Ferrari parked in front of a dry cleaner. After tracking the owner to a nearby phone store, he promptly launched into a narrative of what he could do to fix the minor flaws he noticed on the car. The guy was sold, but he had Kouba detail his wife's BMW first. The customer was then so ecstatic about the quality of the work that Kouba was soon working on the Ferrari. "He has been one of my best customers ever since," he says.

Your Formula for Success

It's easy to see that being an auto detailer takes hard work, persistence, and a sense of humor. Now it's time for you to take your place among the captains of industry. Good luck in your new business venture, and may you make every chassis classy!

Appendix
Automobile Detailing Resources

They say you can never be too rich or too thin. While these could be argued, we believe you can never have too many resources. Therefore, we present for your consideration a wealth of sources for you to check into, check out, and harness for your own personal information blitz. These sources are tidbits, ideas to get you started on your research. They are by no means the only sources out there, and they should not be taken as the Ultimate Answer. We have done our research, but businesses—like customers—tend to move, change, fold, and expand. As we have repeatedly stressed, do your homework. Get out and start investigating.

Associations

Canadian Carwash Association, 649 Queensway W., Mississauga, ON L5B 1C2, CAN, (905) 306–9285, fax: (905) 848–8331, e–mail: office @canadiancarwash.ca, www.canadiancarwash.ca

Central States Carwash Association, 31 E. Berkley Dr., #200, Arlington Heights, IL 60004, (888) 545–9121, fax: (888) 545–9151, e–mail: CSCA carwashpros@aol.com

Heartland Carwash Association, P.O. Box 932, Des Moines, IA 50304, (515) 965–3190, fax: (515) 965–3191, e–mail: heartlandcarwash@aol.com

International Carwash Association, 401 N. Michigan Ave., Chicago, IL 60611, (888) ICA–8422, e–mail: ica@sba.com, www.carcarecentral.com

Mid–Atlantic Carwash Association, The Acumen Group, 2900 Linden Ln., #120, Silver Spring, MD 20910, (310) 962–8000, fax: (301) 495–8870

Midwest Carwash Association, 3225 W. St. Joseph, Lansing, MI 48917, (800) 546–9222, (517) 321–0495, e–mail: midwestcarwash@aol.com, www.midwestcarwash.com

Southeastern Carwash Association, 2690 Valleydale Rd., Birmingham, AL 35244, (800) 834–9706, fax: (205) 991–6771, e–mail: secwa@secwa.com

Southwest Carwash Association, 4600 Spicewood Springs Rd., #103, Austin, TX 78759, (512) 343–9023, fax: (512) 343–1530, e–mail: space@ecpi.com

Western Carwash Association, 10535 Paramount Blvd., #100, Downey, CA 90241, (800) 344–9274, (562) 862–9274, fax: (562) 861–2389, e–mail: wcarwa@aol.com

Business Apparel

Amsterdam Printing, P.O. Box 701, Amsterdam, NY 12010, (800) 833–6231, fax: (518) 843–5204, www.amsterdamprinting.com

Check Verification Services

Electronic Clearing House Inc., 730 Paseo Camarillo, Camarillo, CA 93010, (800) 262–3246, ext. 1, www.echo–inc.com

TeleCheck Services Inc., 5251 Westheimer, #1000, Houston, TX 77056–5251, (800) TELECHECK, (713) 331–7700, fax: (713) 331–7740, www.telecheck.com

Demographic Information

American Demographics, Customer Service, P.O. Box 2042, Marion, OH 43306–8143, (800) 529–7502, www.demographics.com

U.S. Census Bureau, www.census.gov

Detailing Franchises and Licensing Opportunities

The Detail Guys, e–mail: franchiseinfo@detailguys.com, www.detailguys.com

Detail Plus Car Appearance Systems, P.O. Box 20755, Portland, OR 97294, (800) 284–0123, (503) 251–2955, fax: (503) 251–5975, e–mail: info@detailplus.com, www.detailplus.com

Dr. Vinyl, 821 NW Commerce, Lee's Summit, MO 64086, (800) 531–6600, (816) 525–6060, fax: (816) 525–6333, e–mail: tbuckley@drvinyl.com, www.drvinyl.com

FranchiseWorks.com, (877) 824–4411, e–mail: franchiseworks@franchiseworks.com, www. franchiseworks.com

Sparkle Auto, (866) 372–9559, e–mail: info@sparkleauto.com, www.sparkleauto.com

Ziebart International Corp., 1290 E. Maple Rd., P.O. Box 1290, Troy, MI 48007–1290, (800) 877–1312, (248) 588–4100, fax: (248) 588–1444, e–mail: info@ziebart.com, www.ziebart.com

Detailing Systems

Appearance Plus Inc., 4590 Babcock St. NE, #106, Palm Bay, FL 32905, (800) 408–5020, (321) 952–3838, fax: (321) 952–4015, e–mail: info@appearance–plus.com, www.appearance–plus.com

Detail Plus Car Appearance Systems, P.O. Box 20755, Portland, OR 97294, (800) 284–0123, (503) 251–2955, fax: (503) 251–5975, e–mail: info@detailplus.com, www.detailplus.com

National Detail Systems, (800) 356–9485, www.nationaldetail.com

Rightlook.com Inc., 7616 Miramar Rd., #5300, San Diego, CA 92126, (800) 883–3446, (858) 271–4271, fax: (858) 271–4303, e–mail: sales@rightlook.com, www.rightlook.com

Education/Training Resources

Auto Detailing Institute, SMI Research, 108 Ste. B, Eatoncrest Dr., Eatontown, NJ 07724, (732) 544–2142, fax: (732) 544–9047, e–mail: smiresearch@att.net, www.auto detailinginstitute.com

Detail in Progress Inc., P.O. Box 6155, San Diego, CA 92166–0155, (619) 701–1100, fax: (619) 795–2993, e–mail: prentice@detailinprogress.com, www.detailinprogress.com

Detail King, 535 E. Waterfront Dr., #7109, Homestead, PA 15120, (800) 939–6601, fax: (412) 462–9206, e–mail: support@detailking.com, www.detailking.com

Detail Plus Car Appearance Systems, P.O. Box 20755, Portland, OR 97294, (800) 284–0123, (503) 251–2955, fax: (503) 251–5975, e–mail: info@detailplus.com, www.detailplus.com

DriWash 'n Guard, DWG International, (800) 965–7790, e–mail: del@dri–wash.com, www.dri–wash.com

Rightlook.com Inc., 7616 Miramar Rd., #5300, San Diego, CA 92126, (800) 883–3446, (858) 271–4271, fax: (858) 271–4303, e–mail: sales@rightlook.com, www.rightlook.com

Thompson Direct, P.O. Box 1900, Scranton, PA 18501, (800) 275–4410, e–mail: info@ educationdirect.com, www.educationdirect.com

Top of the Line Detailing Supplies, 110 NE Hwy. 45, Bonanza, AR 72916, (800) 533–5743, (479) 638–7302, www.topoftheline.com

Ultimate Auto Detailing Technical Institute, 9600 Lorain Ave., Cleveland, OH 44102, (216) 939–2886, e–mail: detailsupplies@aol.com

Equipment and Supplies

3M, (888) 3M–HELPS, www.3m.com

303 Products Inc., P.O. Box 966, Palo Cedro, CA 96073, (530) 549–5617, fax: (530) 549–5577, e–mail: info@303products.com, www.303products.com

Auto Wax Co. Inc., 1275 Round Table Dr., Dallas, TX 75247, (800) 826–0828, (214) 631–4000, fax: (214) 634–1342, e–mail: info@autowaxcompany.com, www.auto magic.com

Car Brite, 1910 S. State Ave., Indianapolis, IN 46203, (800) 347–2439, (317) 788–9925, fax: (317) 788–9930, e–mail: info@carbrite.com, www.carbrite.com

Clay Magic, Auto Wax Co. Inc., 1275 Round Table Dr., Dallas, TX 75247, (800) 826–0828, (214) 631–4000, fax: (214) 634–1342, e–mail: info@autowaxcompany.com, www. clay–magic.com

ClearKote, P.O. Box 1041, Eufaula, OK 74432, (888) 626–2727, www.clearkote.com

Detail King, 535 E. Waterfront Dr., #7109, Homestead, PA 15120, (800) 939–6601, fax: (412) 462–9206, e–mail: support@detailking.com, www.detailking.com

Detail Plus Car Appearance Systems, P.O. Box 20755, Portland, OR 97294, (800) 284–0123, (503) 251–2955, fax: (503) 251–5975, e–mail: info@detailplus.com, www.detail–plus.com

Forever Black Car Care Products, P.O. Box 6909, Moraga, CA 94570–6909, e–mail: info@foreverblack.com, www.foreverblack.com

Lexol, e–mail: Carolyn@lexol.com, www.lexol.com

Meguiar's Inc., 17991 Mitchell S., Irvine, CA 92614, (800) 347–5700, www.meguiars.com

Pinnacle Car Care Products, (877) WAX–3100, e–mail: info@pinnacle.wax.com, www. pinnaclewax.com

Poorboy's World, (845) 627–5907, e–mail: poorboysworld@att.net, www.poorboys world.com

PremiumAutoCare, Four Star Products Inc., 1813 Seeds Ave., Sarasota, FL 34234, (800) 487–3347, fax: (941) 951–1186, e–mail: sales@premiumautocare.net, www.premiumauto care.com

Professional Dispensing Systems, 883 Parfet St., Lakewood, CO 80215–5548, (888) 386–1247, (303) 238–8343, e–mail: info@pdsweb.net, www.pdsweb.net

Rightlook.com Inc., 7616 Miramar Rd., #5300, San Diego, CA 92126, (800) 883–3446, (858) 271–4271, fax: (858) 271–4303, e–mail: sales@rightlook.com, www.rightlook.com

Top of the Line Detailing Supplies, 110 NE Hwy. 45, Bonanza, AR 72916, (800) 533–5743, (479) 638–7302, www.topoftheline.com

Gift Cards/Certificates

Artemis Solutions Group, 3950 Running Water Dr., Orlando, FL 32829, (800) 331–3921, fax: (360) 331–1072, e–mail: service@smartcardsupply.com, www.smart cardsupply.com

Gift Central, 537 New Britain Ave., Farmington, CT 06034, (800) 283–1695, fax: (800) 428–1951, e–mail: info@giftcentral.com, www.giftcentral.com

Giftworks, 547 Calvin Phillips Dr., Johnson City, TN 37601, (423) 742–0772, e–mail: chuck@ranw.com, www.ranw.com/gresh/Giftworks/orderinginfo.htm

PaperDirect, 1025 E. Woodmen Rd., Colorado Springs, CO 80920, (800) 272–7377, (800) A–PAPERS, fax: (800) 443–2973, (719) 534–1741, e–mail: customerservice@paper direct.com, www.paperdirect.com

Zebra Card Printer Solutions, 1001 Flynn Rd., Camarillo, CA 93012–8706, (800) 452–4056, (805) 579–1800, fax: (805) 579–1808, e–mail: cards@zebra.com, www.eltroncards.com

Incorporation Kits

Inc. Plan USA, Trolley Square, Ste. 26–C, Wilmington, DE 19806, (800) 462–4633, (302) 428–1200, fax: (302) 428–1274, www.incplan.net

Quality Books, 315 SW 50th Ave., Miami, FL 33134, www.qualitybooks.com

Skyweb Enterprises, 3023 Wakefield Dr., Ste. I, Carpentersville, IL 60110, (847) 836–7399, fax: (847) 836–7397, e–mail: webmaster@primeprofits.com, www.primeprof its.com

Merchant Account Services

Merchant Accounts Express, 20–A Northwest Blvd., #102, Nashua, NH 03063, (888) 845–9457, www.merchantexpress.com

MerchantSeek, (800) 233–0406, ext. 5, www.merchantseek.com

Monster Merchant Account Inc., (877) 663–5169, www.monstermerchantaccount.com

Total Merchant Services, 21st Century Resources, DBA Total Merchant Services of Tennessee, 5251–C Hwy. 153, PMB 266, Hixson, TN 37341, (888) 871–4558, (423) 843–2984, fax: (423) 843–9864, e–mail: info@21cr.com, www.merchant–account–4U.com

USA Merchant Account, 22 Ulster Pl., Port Jervis, NY 12771, (866) 828–8683, www.usa–merchantaccount.com

Newsletters

www.carwash.com

www.detail guys.com

www.mobileworks.com

Office Equipment

Beepers.com, 969 2144 Buford Hwy., #111, Buford, GA 30515, (800) BEEPERS, fax: (800) 654–3525, e–mail: info@beepers.com, http://beepers.com

Hello Direct, (800) HELLO–34, e–mail: xpressit@hellodirect.com, www.HelloDirect.com

Office Supplies

Amsterdam Printing, P.O. Box 701, Amsterdam, NY 12010, (800) 833–6231, fax: (518) 843–5204, www.amsterdamprinting.com

Office Depot, www.officedepot.com

Office Max, www.officemax.com

Paper Direct Internet, 1025 E. Woodmen Rd., Colorado Springs, CO 80920, (800) A–PAPERS, fax: (800) 443–2973 e–mail: customerservice@paperdirect.com, www.paperdirect.com

Rapidforms, 301 Grove Rd., Thorofare, NJ 08086–9499, (800) 257–8354, fax: (800) 451–8113, e–mail: service@rapidforms.com, www.rapidforms.com

Staples, www.staples.com

Online Forums/Message Boards

Auto Detailing Secrets of the Experts, www.web–cars.com/detail

Detail City, www.detailcity.com

Meguiar's Online, www.meguiarsonline.com

Mobileworks Auto Detailing and Paintless Dent Repair Forum,www.mobileworks.com

Professional Car Care Online, www.carwash.com

Point–of–Sale Equipment

Credit Card Processing Services, Bailiwick Office Campus, 252 Swamp Rd., Ste. 53–B, Doylestown, PA 18901–2465,(215) 489–7878, fax: (215) 489–7880, e–mail: Kevin@ mcvisa.com, www.mcvisa.com

InfoMerchant Terminal Sales, (800) 603–1399, www.infomerchant.net

Merchant Account Inc., www.creditcard–acceptance.com

Monster Merchant Account Inc., (877) 663–5169, www.monstermerchantaccount.com

Point–of–Sale Software

Chargem, Capital Merchant Solutions Inc., 211 Landmark Dr., Ste. D–4, Normal, IL 61761, (877) 495–2419, (309) 452–5990, fax: (312) 803–1888, e–mail: info@capital merchant.com, www.chargem.com

Credit Card Processing Services, Bailiwick Office Campus, 252 Swamp Rd., Ste. 53–B, Doylestown, PA 18901–2465, (215) 489–7878, fax: (215) 489–7880, e–mail: Kevin@ mcvisa.com, www.mcvisa.com

ICVerify, (800) 666–5777, e–mail: support–icv@icverify.com, www.icverify.com

Merchant Account Express, 20A Northwest Blvd., #102, Nashua, NH 03063, (888) 845–9457, www.merchantexpress.com

PcCharge, GO Software Inc., Parkway Business Center, 5000 Business Center Dr., #1000, Savannah, GA 31405, (877) 659–8984, (912) 527–4400, fax: (912) 527–4531, e–mail: info@gosoftware.com, www.gosoftware.com

POSitive Basic, GO POSitive Software, 2618 N. Columbia Center Blvd., Richland, WA 99352, (800) 735–6860, (509) 735–9194, fax: (419) 781–2197, www.gopositive.com

Printing Resources— Brochures, Door Hangers, Fliers, and Postcards

ColorPrintingCentral, (877) 574–0284, www.colorprintingcentral.com

Printindustry.com, P.O. Box 2238, Ashburn, VA 20146–2238, (703) 631–4533, fax: (703) 729–2268, e–mail: info@printindustry.com, www.printindustry.com

Printing for Less, (800) 930–6040, (406) 222–2689, e–mail: info@printingforless.com, www.printingforless.com

Print Quote USA, 23012B Oxford Pl., Boca Raton, FL 33433, (561) 451–2654, fax: (561) 725–0246, www.printquoteusa.com

Promotion Xpress, (888) 310–7769, e–mail: order@promotionxpress.com, www.promotionxpress.com

PSPrint, 2861 Mandela Pkwy., Oakland, CA 94608, (800) 511–2009, (510) 444–3933, fax: (510) 444–5369, www.psprint.com.

Publications—Consumer

Automobile, P.O. Box 420206, Palm Coast, FL 32142–7446, www.automobilemag.com

AutoWeek, (888) 288–6954, e–mail: awsubs@crain.com, www.autoweek.com

Car & Driver, P.O. Box 52906, Boulder, CO 80322–2906, (850) 682–7654, fax: (303) 604–7644, www.caranddriver.com

Hot Rod, P.O. Box 51397, Boulder, CO 80323–1397, (800) 800–4681, www.hotrod.com

Motor Trend, P.O. Box 420235, Palm Coast, FL 32142–0235, (800) 800–6848, e–mail: motortrend@palmcoastd.com, www.motortrend.com

Mustang Monthly Magazine, P.O. Box 53852, Boulder, CO 80323–3852, (800) 777–6491, e–mail: mustangmonthly@neodata.com, www.mustangmonthly.com

Road & Track, P.O. Box 55279, Boulder, CO 80322–5279, (850) 682–7654, fax: (303) 604–7644, e–mail: Rd.andtrack@neodata.com, www.roadandtrack.com

Truck Trend, (800) 274–1971, e–mail: trucktrend@palmcoastd.com, www.trucktrend.com

Vette, McMullen Argus Publishing Inc., 2400 E. Katella Ave., 11th Fl., Anaheim, CA 92806, (714) 939–2400, fax: (714) 978–6390, www.vetweb.com

Publications—Detailing Business

America's Car Care Business, P.O. Box 25310, Scottsdale, AZ 85255–9998, (480) 585–0455, fax: (480) 585–0456

Auto Laundry News, EW Williams Publications Co., 2125 Center Ave., #305, Fort Lee, NJ 07024–5898, (201) 592–7007, fax: (201) 592–7171, www.carwashingmag.com

Detailers Digest, P.O. Box 5950, Clearwater, FL 33758–5950, (727) 531–7885, fax: (727) 531–7850, e–mail: SunKingPub@aol.com

Mobile–Tech News & Views, P.O. Box 5950, Clearwater, FL 33758–5950, (727) 531–7885, fax: (727) 531–7850, e–mail: MTNEWSVWS@aol.com

Modern Car Care, Virgo Publishing Inc. 3300 N. Central Ave., Phoenix, AZ 85012, (480) 990–1101, ext. 1285, fax: (480) 990–0819, www.moderncarcare.com

Professional Carwashing & Detailing, National Trade Publications Inc., 13 Century Hill Dr., Latham, NY 12110–2197, (518) 783–1281, ext. 3167, fax: (518) 783–1386, www.carwash.com

Safety Equipment

Omark Safety, 3505 104th St., Des Moines, IA 50322, (515) 278–5422, fax: (515) 278–5702,e–mail: sales@omarksafety.com, www.omarksafety.com

Safety Glasses USA Inc., P.O. Box 1021, Three Rivers, MI 49093, (800) 870–6189, www.safetyglassesusa.com

Successful Automobile Detailers

Duncan, Karen, Union Park Appearance Care Center, Wilmington, DE, e–mail: LovYourCar@aol.com

Echnoz, Dave, 14/69 Carwash Supercenter, 714 Ave. of Autos, Fort Wayne, IN 46804, (260) 436–9274, fax: (260) 434–4990, e–mail: carwashsupercenter@hotmail.com, www.1469carwash.com

Kouba, Gary, Perfect Auto Finish, (630) 947–2090, e–mail: Gary@PerfectAutoFinish.com, www.perfectautofinish.com

Myers, Mike, Gem Auto Appearance Center, 11750 Pika Dr., Waldorf, MD 20602, (301) 645–2415, fax: (310) 645–0412, e–mail: PolishYourBoat@aol.com

Orosco, Anthony, Ultimate Reflections, 6210 Cherrywest, San Antonio, TX 78240, (210) 641–0752, e–mail: ultimatereflections@msn.com, www.ultimatereflections.net

St. Clair, Prentice, Detail in Progress Inc., P.O. Box 6155, San Diego, CA 92166–0155, (619) 701–1100, fax: (619) 795–2993, e–mail: prentice@detailinprogress.com, www.detailinprogress.com

Schurmann, Tom, Professional Detailing Systems, 883 Parfet St., Lakewood, CO 80215–5548, (303) 238–8343, e–mail: info@pdsweb.net, www.pdsweb.net

▲

Trade Shows

Car Care World Expo, International Carwash Association, (888) ICA–8422, e–mail: ica@sba.com

Midwest Carwash Association Expo, Midwest Carwash Association, 3225 W. St. Joseph, Lansing, MI 48917, (800) 546–9222, (517) 321–0495, e–mail: midwestcarwash@aol.com, www.midwestcarwash.com

Mobile Tech Expo, P.O. Box 5950, Clearwater, FL 33758–5950, (727) 531–7885, fax: (727) 531–7850, e–mail: mobileexpo@aol.com, www.mobiletechexpo.com

Water Reclamation Systems

Top of the Line Detailing Supplies, 110 NE Hwy. 45, Bonanza, AR 72916, (800) 533–5743, (479) 638–7302, www.topoftheline.com

Web Hosting/Domain Names

Apollo Hosting, 2303 Ranch Rd. 620 S., #135–301, Austin, TX 78734, (877) 525–HOST, (512) 261–1203, www.apollohosting.com

DOMAIN.com., (800) 583–3382, www.domain.com

EarthLink, (800) 201–8615, www.earthlink.net

iPowerWeb, 2800 28th St., #205, Santa Monica, CA 90405, (888) 511–HOST, e–mail: sales@ipowerweb.com, www.ipowerweb.com

NetPass, 419 N. Magnolia Ave., Orlando, FL 32801, (407) 843–7277, fax: (407) 843–2105, e–mail: sales@netpass.com, www.netpass.com

Webhosting.com, (888) WEBHOST, e–mail: sales@webhosting.com, www.webhosting.com

Yahoo!, (866) 781–9246, http://webhosting.yahoo.com

Glossary

Acid rain: rain that contains airborne contaminants and emissions (including sulfuric acid) from fossil fuel–burning plants, vehicles, and other sources that will etch vehicle paint finishes if not removed.

Air compressor: a device for powering pneumatic tools.

Black trim restoration: the process of restoring faded vinyl and rubber molding and trim.

Bonnet: used on an orbital polisher to remove cleaners, polish, wax, and other sealants.

Brake dust: the particles produced by a vehicle's brake pads as they rub against the rotor.

Brochure: a printed sales piece outlining your company's services and capabilities.

Carnauba wax: one of the hardest waxes available; works best when combined with other types of wax.

Carpet extractor: a device for pulling shampoo and rinse water out of carpet.

Cement removal: removal of cement particles or film from vehicle paint and trim.

▲

Chamois: a type of leather that has been tanned to make it soft.

Chat room: an electronic "gathering place" on the internet for people who share special interests, where they can exchange information, comment, or commiserate about topics of mutual interest in real time.

Claying: the process of using a clay bar (similar to Play–Doh) to remove contaminants from the surface of paint after a vehicle is washed and dried.

Clearcoat: a protective coating over the base coating of paint that protects the color from oxidizing.

Contingency fee: a payment for legal services that is a percentage of a settlement (frequently 25 percent or higher).

Cutting/finishing pad: used on a rotary buffer/polisher to correct surface irregularities in paint or to polish paint to a high shine.

dba: "doing business as;" refers to the name you choose for your business, even if it has your own name in it (as in Dave's Auto Detailing and Car Spa).

Demographics: the primary characteristics of your target audience, such as age, gender, ethnic background, income level, education level, and home ownership.

Detailing clay: a product used to remove surface contamination, like particles and paint overspray, from a vehicle's painted surfaces.

Dressing: the process of applying cleaning/conditioning products.

Electronic business card: a static page on a web site that gives little more than a business's contact information, including a phone number to call for more information.

Ergonomic: scientifically designed for the comfort and safety of the people who use it (for example, an ergonomic chair).

Express detailing: an appearance–care service completed within 15 minutes after vehicle washing; often includes vacuuming, cleaning/dressing of interior surfaces, and other detailing processes.

Feature article: an article that goes into more detail than a newspaper or other journalistic news story.

Flash: an electronic file format for delivering graphics and/or animation on the internet; also known as Shockwave Flash.

Fogger odor remover: a product used to neutralize and destroy odors, especially in carpet, velour, leather, and vinyl, as well as ventilation systems; also commonly known as "odor bombs."

Freelancer: a self–employed person who works on a project or contract basis.

Goldplating: the application of gold finish to automotive chrome and stainless steel; often used to recondition or give a new look to vehicle emblems.

Headliner: the fabric that lines a vehicle's ceiling.

Icon: a symbol on a web site that links the user to specific information.

Independent contractor: see "freelancer."

Indicia: in bulk mailing, the box that appears in place of a postage stamp, which gives information about the mail type (i.e., first class, bulk postage rate), a permit number (for the account into which postage money was deposited), and the place where the mailing "dropped," or was sent from.

Interactive: in computer language, characterized by an exchange of data between the computer user and a host, like an internet web site.

Logo (or logotype): an identifying symbol used by organizations.

Loupe: a photographer's tool that detailers use to detect or examine flaws in paint.

Masking: covering up the paint, chrome, fabric, or other materials next to the area of the vehicle being worked on to prevent damage; often done with masking tape alone or with newspaper affixed with masking tape.

Media card: the card used in a digital camera to store photographs.

Overspray removal: removal of chemical contaminants like asphalt, tar, concrete, industrial fallout, and paint deposited on vehicle paint and trim.

Ozone odor remover: an air purification device that removes odors caused by smoke, mold, fungi, and bacteria.

Paint leveler: a product used to remove grit scratches without leaving swirls.

Paint thickness gauge: a device that measures the thickness of paint to determine how thick the clearcoat is.

Paintless dent repair: a technique that removes door dings and hail damage from automotive finishes.

Polish: a paint conditioner used to restore oil to automotive paint, remove fine scratches, and create high gloss; compare to "wax."

Pressure washer: a device for delivering water under high pressure; also used for applying cleaning products.

Quality–of–finish measurement instrument: a device for measuring and evaluating automotive finishes.

Rail dust: iron dust particles created by friction between train wheels and train tracks that settle on the finish of vehicles transported by rail, which then corrode and become embedded in the finish.

Random orbital polisher: a power tool used for buffing and shampooing; operates in an irregular circular pattern.

Real time: in computer lingo, "as it happens;" this means you can respond immediately to a message posted on a bulletin board or in a chat room.

Rotary buffer/polisher: tool for correcting surface irregularities on paint and/or polishing paint to a high shine; it doesn't apply torque to the surface and operates in a random pattern.

Sand trap/oil separator: type of sewage equipment that removes pollutants from water generated by businesses like detailers before the water is discharged into the sewer system.

Swirl marks: fine scratches in a circular pattern on vehicle finishes caused by using a buffer incorrectly.

Tag line: a slogan used to build audience recognition for a service or product.

Tank sprayer: a pressurized container for delivering chemicals.

Teaser: a clever line of copy, often on the outside of an envelope, which entices the audience to read further.

Temperature gauge: a device for checking the surface temperature of paint.

Wastewater reclamation system: equipment used to contain and capture wastewater and chemical runoff from detailing operations.

Wax: a substance used to protect a vehicle's shine; applied after polish.

Wet–dry vac: a less expensive alternative to a carpet extractor.

Index

▲

The Only Start-up Book You'll Ever Need!

Each month, millions of established and aspiring entrepreneurs turn to Rieva Lesonsky and the staff of *Entrepreneur* magazine to learn how to start a business. So what are you waiting for? Pick up a copy today.

The third edition of *Start Your Own Business* walks you through every step of the start-up process and is packed with advice and information on new topics, such as:

- How to Get New Business Ideas
- Secrets to Getting Government Grants
- How the Internet Can Boost Your Business
- Tips for Starting a Nonprofit Organization
- Updated "Hot Links" to Relevant Web Sites

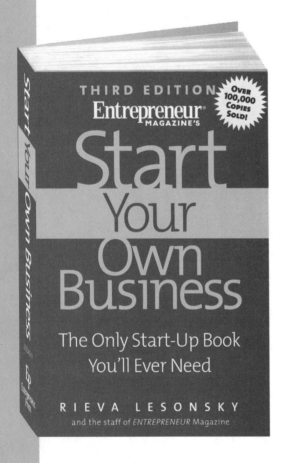

THIRD EDITION
Entrepreneur MAGAZINE'S
OVER 100,000 COPIES SOLD!

Start Your Own Business

The Only Start-Up Book You'll Ever Need

RIEVA LESONSKY
and the staff of *ENTREPRENEUR* Magazine

> "*Entrepreneur* has created a superb resource for successfully getting your business off the ground."
> – Fred DeLuca, Founder, Subway Restaurants

PHOTO©DAVIS BARBER

A nationally recognized speaker and expert on small business and entrepreneurship with more than 20 years of experience in journalism, bestselling author Rieva Lesonsky and her staff have helped hundreds of thousands of entrepreneurs achieve their dreams.

Pick up your copy today!

AVAILABLE AT ALL FINE BOOKSTORES AND ONLINE BOOKSELLERS | WWW.ENTREPRENEURPRESS.COM

EP
Entrepreneur Press